THE
WARRIOR
THE
STRATEGIST
AND
YOU

THE
WARRIOR
THE
STRATEGIST
AND
YOU

HOW TO FIND YOUR PURPOSE & REALISE YOUR POTENTIAL

FLOYD WOODROW

First published 2016 by
Elliott and Thompson Limited
27 John Street
London WC1N 2BX
www.eandtbooks.com

ISBN: 978-1-78396-273-0

9 8 7 6 5 4 3

A catalogue record for this book is available from the British Library.

Illustrations: Chantal Dean
Typesetting: Marie Doherty
Printed in the UK by TJ International Ltd

Contents

Introduction   vii

Chapter 1: Finding our Super North Star   1
Chapter 2: Establishing our starting point   25
Chapter 3: Our Ethos   41
Chapter 4: The Strategist   63
Chapter 5: The Warrior   97
Chapter 6: Our Compass for Life in action   133
Chapter 7: Working as a team   165

Conclusion   195
Acknowledgements   201
Bibliography and Further Reading   205
Index   207

Introduction

Are you reaching your full potential in life?

This book is a gateway: it will show you how to do just that. It will help you understand what your potential really is and how to release it. With simple adjustments to your approach to life, you can better succeed in your dreams and ambitions. These concepts will be easy to apply to any of your endeavours, for the rest of your life, and you'll be able to pass them on to others as well.

My fascination with human potential, and how we can release and harness it, has been a key driver throughout my life. I was fortunate to be a soldier for over twenty-seven years, most of them in the SAS, working with talented, dynamic and entrepreneurial people who happened also to be elite soldiers. I've studied psychology and philosophy and worked with people from all walks of life and cultures, exploring how we engage with others, how we achieve for ourselves and, more importantly, at our highest level, for society.

When we look at the lives of our heroes, we see that they had to overcome misfortune, external resistance, jealousy, stubbornness, failure and mistrust. We are no different from them; we all have storms to weather. I judge the performance of a person or team when I see them at the height of the storm's fury, working through adversity and coming out the other side intact and together. Because success is achieved through strategy; failure is not an accident. We sometimes assume that success is bestowed upon the lucky few, but the truth is that it is much less about luck or chance, and more about hard work and dedication; knowing what we want, how to get there and having the courage and determination to make it happen.

I have had many different roles in my life: soldier, boxer, businessman, father, negotiator, author and others in between. Each role has helped me understand the four elements in life that can help me to succeed. I think of these elements in terms of a compass – my Compass for Life. My Super North Star is the north cardinal on my compass, the essence of who I am and my purpose; it energises me, draws me forward and I am passionate about achieving it. The south point is my Strategist, my ability to plan my life and build the scaffolding I need to get to my Super North Star. East is my Ethos – my values, my behaviour, the things I believe in, and they are non-negotiable on my journey to achieving my purpose. West is my Warrior, my strength of character and desire to fight for what I want and believe.

It is important to keep our compass points balanced – over-relying on any one aspect can hold us back. Having a warrior spirit is less effective when it is not backed up with a clear strategy, something I know only too well, having allowed my warrior side to dominate my approach for many years. But when we are moving forward with all of our compass points in equilibrium, then we really can achieve whatever we put our minds to.

With our compass in hand, we now need our map to follow. Visualising a 'life map' is a helpful way to stay focused on our goals: we look at the routes we may have to travel, the obstacles we have to navigate and the steps we need to take to get to our destination. We should jot all of this down, using pictures as well as words, so that they are no longer just ideas in our mind, but start to form an actual drawn-out map, one that we can return to for direction and inspiration, and add to throughout our journey.

Once our mind, body and spirit are connected and triangulated, we will have the power to succeed in any area of life we choose. My wish is for this book to touch, inspire and empower you, so that you develop a clear idea of where you want to go, who you want to be, and what you need to do to succeed. I will tell my story as though we were in the same room, and I will tell the truth; it will be a journey we'll travel together. The stories I tell of others will also be true, although names will, of course, have been changed to protect their privacy.

'Things should be made as simple as possible, not simpler.'
ALBERT EINSTEIN

I recommend that you first read the whole book from cover to cover. At the end of each chapter, there is a series of exercises, which you should read through on your first pass, but do not undertake them until you have an overview of the whole book. Then return to those sections to complete the exercises.

Use the book as a notebook for your ideas – please write in it, scribble over it, sketch in it, annotate it, index key paragraphs or chapters to keep you on track. I hope it becomes something you return to time and again, to remind you of your true potential.

Above all, I want you to trust in yourself, commit to your future and seize the opportunity to push the boundaries of your potential.

The futurist writer Alvin Toffler once said: 'The very process of writing changes me. It clarifies my thoughts. It organises my time and my life.'

Writing this book has made me explore my theories, challenge my beliefs and put into words my thoughts on how we can push through our limitations to achieve what we desire. It has made me reflect back on the lessons I have learned throughout my life and how they have shaped me; I will share those lessons with you in these pages, and I hope that they will motivate you. There are early childhood experiences that had a great impact on me – you may find some are similar to your own; stories from my time in the SAS – probably a less common experience, but hopefully more inspiring; and finally, my time spent teaching, during which I've had the privilege of working with some of the most talented people in the world in the fields of sports, business, the military and education.

The concepts in this book are designed to be easy to understand and easy to apply to your own life, whatever your circumstances, whatever your ambitions. They will enable you to explore your own ideas, encourage you to change the way you think about your performance and help you to start working towards your goals. It is an honour to share them with you.

Have fun,
Floyd

Chapter 1

Finding our Super North Star

The first step towards our Compass for Life is working out our direction in life. This is our Super North Star: an unambiguous statement of intent, a purpose to aim towards. Otherwise we risk simply drifting through life – a risk not worth taking by anyone. But how do we find our purpose, and how do we go about achieving it?

As a boy, and even as a man, I spent a lot of time day-dreaming. Despite being told at school to 'concentrate' and 'pay attention, Floyd!', I never lost the habit, which is for-tunate, because those people were wrong. Daydreaming is increasingly being understood as necessary to creative and personal development. Although we do have to pick our moment – letting our imagination wander while on a long walk, good; letting our imagination wander while operating behind enemy lines, bad.

Over the years I have dreamed of being rich, of being a PE teacher (there is no logic to dreaming), of driving a sports car, of being a soldier, a successful businessman, a professional sportsman, a leading barrister, a bestselling author, a pilot – the list goes on, even to this day.

I have also had to accept that some of my dreams are beyond me. I am never going to be a singer, for example, and the less said about the boy band my friends and I set up,

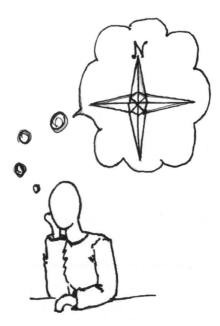

the better. (We got it to the audition stage before someone told us we were rubbish. Thank God there was no *X Factor* in my day, but you can't say we didn't try.)

I have recently worked with a number of children and young adults from the ages of five to eighteen. The first question I asked them was, 'What are your dreams and ambitions?' As soon as they were allowed to think about this without limits, solutions, timelines or judgement, they came up with wonderful ideas, ones that were challenging and scary. For many of them it was the first time they felt safe to tell people about their Super North Star, without the fear of someone ridiculing them, or telling them to be realistic, or telling them that they have no chance of success or are not talented enough. Our dreams and ambitions can be fragile to start with, which is why we need something or someone to unlock them and allow them to grow, not extinguish them.

'At the age of six, I wanted to be a cook. At seven, I wanted to be Napoleon. And my ambition has been growing steadily ever since.'

SALVADOR DALÍ

The fearlessness of a child's imagination is a wonder to behold; they'll happily see themselves as an astronaut, superhero or lion king, with no limitations. Sadly, for most people, dreams stop after childhood. Hope, imagination, excitement and joy are replaced with a plodding sense of compromise called 'reality', where dreams are tamped down rather than treasured and upheld.

Any idea can suddenly inspire us, so it's important never to give up daydreaming – it allows us to explore what it is we really want in life, to help us find our purpose. And we must have a purpose; life is too short to waste. Passion inspires our minds and touches our hearts and drives us forward. So beware if you are in a job that you hate; it will likely limit what you can achieve in it.

The power of purpose

The 'power of purpose' is very important. Once, after I had given a talk on this topic, I asked a young woman what her purpose was. She said she was doing a biology degree and was thinking of going into pharmaceuticals, 'because that's where the money is'. Then her face lit up as she continued with her story: 'But my real love is the environment.' She explained how important it was to her with such passion, warmth and energy. I raised my eyebrows and she smiled; she knew what her purpose in life was.

'Don't ask yourself what the world needs. Ask yourself what makes you come alive and go do it, because what the world needs is people who have come alive.'

HOWARD THURMAN

We should be able to answer the question of why we are doing what we're doing to anyone who asks. Our purpose can be personal, professional or social. If it can encapsulate all three, we really will have a life worth living.

Nurturing our dreams

The seeds for my Super North Star were planted when I was still just a long-limbed boy. As my skinny frame started to harden, the idea began to take shape in my mind. I was destined for the army. Seeing my older brother in his Royal Marines uniform helped. And my childhood hero was Alexander the Great – not a made-up superhero, but a real man, who fought for what he believed, who led his men from the front, and who achieved incredible things, all before he was thirty-two years old. These sources of inspiration fed into my desire to be a soldier. What I really wanted in life was to see how good I could be, both physically and mentally. I wanted to be tested and challenged, and I knew the army was the place for that. My Super North Star continued to grow and my strategy started to take shape. I understood the milestones I would need to hit along the way, and I realised that to truly test my potential it was the Parachute Regiment I needed to join, and then the SAS, until it was all I wanted to do.

My dream was only a flicker when I encountered the first obstacle, which was that nobody supported or believed in me. My careers teacher was particularly scathing about my desire to join the army and my ability to join the SAS. However, my resolve was such that this was only a minor blip on my journey, one of a number I would encounter and overcome before joining the Parachute Regiment on 2 February 1981.

Adapting our purpose

As important as it is to stay focused on our Super North Star, our journey is not always clear-cut. Sometimes our circumstances change, we change, what's important to us changes, and we need a new purpose to pursue. We need to be adaptable – if we're not flexible enough to change direction when needed, we may miss valuable opportunities. The key is making sure we're making the right decision – changing our Super North Star because it's the right thing for us, not just giving up on the challenge we set ourselves because it has become difficult.

I was once running an eleven-week training exercise for a team I had just taken over. I had been in 'the trees' (jungle) for over six weeks, live-firing, patrolling, setting ambushes, conducting navigation exercises. The next morning was to be the culmination of a tough two-week training exercise for this particular team: a live camp attack. It had been raining for hours, so, although the canopy was dense, the floor of the jungle was sodden and muddy. The thunder in the distance meant it was not going to abate. *Tomorrow will be a tough day*, I mused to myself.

At the time, I was also in the third year of my law degree, so here I was, in the pitch black, as only the jungle can be at night, but for the torch on my head, huddled over my law books, braced against the chill in the air. I was alone; everyone had now gone to bed in preparation for the busy day tomorrow. I had an essay on criminal law to finish, to be sent out in the morning by helicopter.

When I'd first thought about changing direction and leaving the SAS, I thought a degree would help and I chose law. A barrister looked like a great career – I imagined the cut and thrust of being in a courtroom. And, after all, I'd had some experience of being on the wrong side of such proceedings (although I was innocent – I'd stepped into a fight to help a friend who was being attacked by a group of men).

As I finished the last few sentences of my essay, I was drawn back to two books I'd been reading, one on the mind and psychology, the other on communication strategies, negotiation and leadership. I suddenly had a flash of inspiration about my future. I was going to finish my law degree, but I was not going to become a barrister. I was going to become a teacher of leadership and performance. I was going to learn more about psychology and use this knowledge to enhance, from an academic perspective, what I had learned from experience and see where that took me. As I have previously said, when I was young I had wanted to be a PE teacher – clearly my desire to teach had not been lost.

Although this was only a flicker of a thought, the debate in my mind began immediately; whether to stick with my chosen Super North Star or abandon it for this new direction, and I began to identify the pros and cons. Four years of hard work against my desire to teach. In many cases this can be a battle between safety (staying with what we know) and our desire to push our potential (take a risk) and achieve something in life. I wondered if I was avoiding becoming a barrister and staying as a soldier because it was safe? I needed to delve a little deeper before I finally decided.

I loved being a soldier and knew I could have several more years learning and growing in the army, but I knew I couldn't do that job for ever. I was unsure, however, about finding a role I'd love as much as my current one. Throughout my adult life, the army had been my primary source of identity. With a lot of people, when you ask them what they do, you know that their answer – I drive a forklift truck, I work in a supermarket, I'm a salesman, I'm a director, etc – is just that, it's what they do; it's not who they are. With me, it was. I was a soldier first and foremost. It suited my temperament, my abilities, my philosophy and my physical type. I was passionate about it and never compromised, not once. If our purpose in life is so important to us, I felt uneasy about giving up mine for the unknown. All I knew was I didn't want to stay or do something just because it was comfortable.

Ultimately, I finished my degree, so I didn't give up on something I'd already started, but I chose to pursue teaching over becoming a lawyer. I realised that law was never my true passion, just one of the many things I decided to try while searching for my next Super North Star. When we're not sure what our purpose is in life, setting ourselves goals and taking little steps forward can help us see things more clearly and decide what it is that is important to us. The extra skills and experience I gained through my law degree have been invaluable to me and, more importantly, led me to my new purpose. Teaching was a much more fulfilling goal; I knew the instant the thought took hold in my mind that adapting my goal was the correct decision, and I have never regretted it.

Set the bar high

Our purpose should be challenging, it should be one that is worth achieving. We should make sure that we are aiming high enough, that we are pushing ourselves to achieve, and that we are reaching our full potential. If we set ourselves easy goals, we'll never truly excel and discover exactly how much we are capable of achieving.

And when setting tough targets, it's important to always believe in ourselves. We shouldn't let others deter us from our purpose. I can't begin to tell you how many times I have been told I couldn't achieve something, but that sort of negative response only seemed to strengthen my resolve.

It began with boxing, which I was nearly put off from even starting. When I excitedly asked a teacher if I could enrol in a competition, he just laughed and told me to come back when I was tougher and had more weight on me. He practically ruffled my hair and said 'Run along, sonny'. I kept my devastation to myself and it took six full months of inner turmoil before I summoned enough courage to think 'Sod you!' and step into a boxing ring to fight.

I realised quite quickly I liked people telling me I couldn't do something. It meant I knew I'd set myself a real challenge and it also motivated me to succeed.

We shouldn't let anyone take our dreams from us. Our dreams should be big and scary; when people tell us we aren't going to succeed then we know we've got a Super North Star worth striving for.

'A man's reach should exceed his grasp, or what's a heaven for?'
ROBERT BROWNING

Seizing inspiration

Sometimes I am asked 'What if you really do not know where your Super North Star is, Floyd?' Strangely, though, my experience of this, even with children, is rare.

My answer is to undertake as many experiences as we can to draw us forward. We never know what might inspire our purpose – a long-held dream or an idle thought – so we should always be open to ideas. I've worked with people for whom a simple, random thought one day sparked a new way of thinking and revealed their true direction. The key is to take the time to allow the thought in and then catch it before it disappears by writing it down – even if the idea isn't fully formed yet. We should trust our intuition and allow it to find ways to tell us where we should go. We should listen to our emotions, think about those things in life we are passionate about and energised by, and know that we are unique and that the things we dream about will be within our capability – as long as we commit to them.

My son has just decided upon his Super North Star at the age of twenty-seven, after trying numerous activities including being a lifeguard, surfer and financial-sector worker. He is now going to become a soldier. This has actually always been his Super North Star, but before he committed to it he wanted to make sure it was what he wanted by trying other things and gaining other experiences first. He also wanted to make sure he was not being influenced by me and my experiences in the army. And there is nothing wrong with that: we shouldn't feel we have to rush into our decisions. There is a difference between procrastinating and taking the time to really consider our choices. If we're not ready to commit to an idea, we should be sure to take small steps forward and, with time and experience, our purpose will gradually become clearer.

'Your work is to discover your world and then with all your heart to give yourself to it.'

BUDDHA

When I was unsure what I would do after leaving the military, I did anything that took my fancy. I took a law degree, learned some languages, studied psychology, wrote a book. I tend to get caught up in the excitement of a new challenge quite quickly and it consumes all my energy and focus, so I have to be quite careful which ideas I choose to pursue these days. My desire to be a soldier started as a simple thought and went on to consume half my life; flying was an idle dream in my childhood but I found I couldn't stop until I had done it; I enrolled on the law course after just one conversation with a friend; and my current desire – to fly a helicopter – nips at me every time I think about it. But, finally, all of these experiences have led me to my new Super North Star: I want to build an international leadership academy, teaching children and adults the skills they need to succeed in their endeavours.

And of course there will be more; there are always more.

'Insight is not a light bulb that goes off inside our heads. It is a flickering candle that can easily be snuffed out.'

MALCOLM GLADWELL

Compass for Life

Once we have found our Super North Star, we need a way to navigate towards it. What better way to find north than with our own compass?

I can still remember my first actual compass. I'd just joined the Paras and how to use it was one of our first lessons. It sat in my hand, a Silva compass: an oblong of plastic, etched with numbers, a red and white needle in a dial; ancient but modern, incomprehensible but fascinating. It had a magnifier, milli-metre and inch scales, a bezel marked in degrees, and strange angular markings, which I soon learned were Romer scales of 1:25.000 and 1:50.000, with which you could find the exact location of anything on a map. It was, in its own way, thrilling.

Our navigation and location skills were constantly tested during my time in the Paras, and the importance of getting it right drilled into us again and again. We were taught how to break our journey down into sections, and plot the bearing of each one. We learned how to read the contours of the land, how steep a route would be, what obstacles we might meet, the type of terrain we'd have to cross, where we would ren-dezvous and where our targets were. And alongside this we learned about the magnetic variation and how to take it into account. There are no small mistakes in map reading – a lapse in concentration can easily take you miles off track. I used a compass throughout my military career, and the same basic truth remains: the compass does not lie, as one of my mentors in the Paras, Al Slater, used to point out. We may misinterpret the information, the map may be faulty, and the ground may have changed, but the compass will always point north. As long as we've plotted our route correctly, it will guide us on our journey.

I remember a march in the Brecon Beacons when I was training for the SAS. A number of us were training alongside one another, testing out different routes. One of the marches took five hours if you made it in time, much longer if you took the wrong route. The mist came down on my way to the final checkpoint. Time was getting tight and, stumbling along, unable to see more than a few feet in front of me, I had to take all my bearings from my compass. Suddenly, out of the mist, came a figure I recognised as a friend. He was a much better map reader than I was, and he was headed in a slightly different direction en route to the final checkpoint. We stopped to talk and I told him which way my compass was pointing, and he said he knew the terrain, had been there before and was confident he knew the way. I was uneasy, but my mentor's voice kicked in, quietly but certain: 'The compass does not lie, trust it. It always points north.' We parted and, although I still felt uneasy along the route, I arrived at the checkpoint thirty minutes ahead of him.

It is why I now have my life compass. When we have the correct information for our journey, and are passionate and committed, it will always point us in the correct direction. Our paths to success are never as smooth as we have planned, but if we have a clear and dedicated goal, with the right approach, we will always be able to keep our Super North Star in sight, no matter what obstacles life throws in our way.

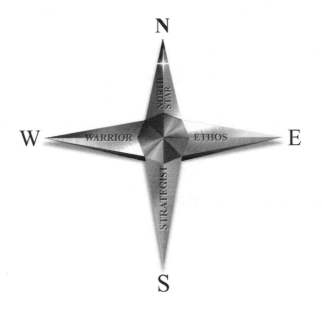

The picture on the previous page encapsulates the elements in our Compass for Life. North is our Super North Star. That is where we are trying to get to. Understanding and aligning the rest of the points on our compass will help us get there.

The east cardinal is our Ethos: our values, behaviour and character. It is our emotional intelligence, the essence of who we are, both as individuals and as a team. Our ethos needs to be aligned to our purpose. It will be tested on difficult journeys and we will need to be courageous and accountable for our beliefs. This is vitally important when we are part of a team, because it becomes our agreed team code of conduct, our way of working together. If we do not have a decent and honourable ethos, it will overshadow whatever we may achieve, as many people have found to their cost.

The south symbol is our Strategy. As strategists, we must analyse all the information available, without emotion, and carefully plan our options, making sure we are realistic in setting milestones to get to our Super North Star.

West is our Warrior Spirit. This is our strength of character to get to each milestone, being disciplined, focused, relentless and determined. Looking after our physical fitness and practising the basic skills we need until they are second nature.

Once we have our compass, we can start to look at the terrain we will have to cross.

Creating a life map

Visualising what we want to achieve, creating our own map for our journey, is also vitally important as it focuses our mind. I have kept a notebook for as long as I can remember, to record what I've learned, observed and felt, and also what questions I have, things I need to avoid doing and so on. I capture inspirational quotes and poems and I draw symbols, pictures or doodles that mean something to me (I am not a perfect artist, by any means, but I am the only one who needs to see the drawings). It's a map of my life, my journey both inner and outer, and I enjoy looking back on it. Keeping it has helped me and the practice has benefited many other people who have risen to the top of their profession as well. Over time I have developed it further and on the next page is my current map towards my current Super North Star, showing my journey to date.

My first Super North Star, which sits in the left-hand corner of the picture, was to join the Parachute Regiment. Then came the Special Air Service; during that time I was happy with what I was doing, but I decided to learn a lot of different skills as I knew that I would eventually do something different. And now my new Super North Star is my leadership academy, which sits in the top right-hand corner of the picture.

When we can visualise our dreams and ambitions and put them down on paper, something magical happens. Our dreams become more focused and real. Felix Baumgartner drew a picture for his mum when he was five years old that showed him parachuting high in the sky above mountains and he went on to complete the highest-ever skydive from the edge of space. Jonny Wilkinson wrote a letter as a nine-year-old about wanting to play rugby for his school's first team and then for England.

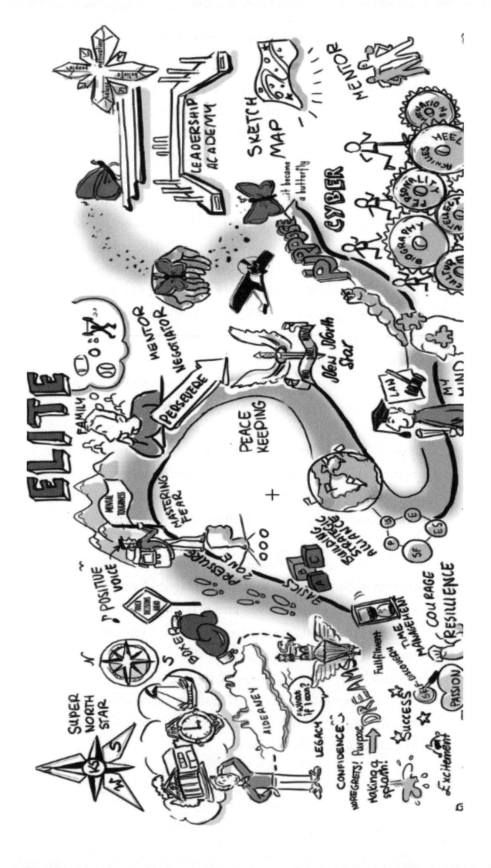

'Imagination is more important than knowledge.'

ALBERT EINSTEIN

I recently spoke with a young girl who told me how she visualises her Compass for Life: she sees herself as her own Super North Star; her Ethos is a mirror; her Strategist is a chess piece; and for her Warrior, she pictures Athena. Having such strong mental pictures of a concept can really bring it to life, and help us to understand and commit to it more fully.

By consciously defining our Ethos, Strategist and Warrior cardinals, we can remain true to our purpose. By looking at our map we become more attuned to the actions we need to take and more determined to achieve our purpose. Our map becomes almost like a contract with ourselves, one that we don't want to break. The key is combining all of these definitions into our approach; once they are aligned we will have the passion, motivation, desire and energy to fuel our purpose. This becomes our Compass for Life; when our cardinal points are in perfect balance, we will always be able to find our way.

We will take a look at each of the cardinal points in turn in later chapters. The most important part of any life story, though, especially our own, is finding our Super North Star, so that is where we will begin. Once we have our Super North Star in our mind's eye, we can start to draw our own map to ensure we stay on track.

Points for action: identifying your Super North Star

Find yourself a piece of paper. Sit quietly, take a deep breath and think about having a Super North Star, without placing any limitations. Think about this from an individual perspective first. Ask yourself: 'Does my life have a purpose I'm happy with?' Let your thoughts flow; don't limit them with doubt, censor them, or allow your inner voice, or anyone else's, to crush them. This is a time to imagine and wonder how good could you actually be.

If a powerful thought emerges, something that catches your attention, embrace it. It doesn't have to be a fully formed idea at this stage. Start to draw it; you do not have to be an artist; this is just for you. Think about the things you want to achieve, the person you will be and the environment you want to work in. Think about the team around you (if there is a team), your family, the skills you have or need. Draw symbols, use words, sketch and use bright colours – these don't have to be coherent pictures. Sometimes people struggle to begin with, but once you start to draw you will be amazed at what happens as your dreams become a little more real.

I have done this exercise with all kinds of people, from the toughest soldiers in the world to small children and every sector in between. The comments I have heard most often include: 'it helps declutter my mind'; 'it now becomes real'; 'this morning I would have told you that I do not know what I want to become, but now I do and I am excited about it'. Your map simply starts to open the gateway to your Super North Star. You should keep returning to this map to add in any other thoughts and ideas that the rest of this book may inspire. Indeed, keep returning and adding to it throughout your lifetime as your goals, ideas and inspirations change.

While you are in a reflective mood, continue to ask yourself other questions related to your future and your purpose to keep the creative thoughts flowing. If you are still stuck, think about the following questions:

☛ What did you dream of being and doing in your life when you were in primary school and how did this differ when you went to secondary school and later in life – and why?

☛ What are the wildest options you have thought of pursuing?

☛ What do you need most of all at this moment in time?

☛ In a perfect world what job would you do?

☛ What do you currently do that inspires you, during work or leisure time?

☛ What gets you out of bed in the morning and energises you?

☛ Who are your heroes and heroines and why?

☛ What experiences would you like to have in life?

Once you have thought about your answers to these questions, look at your patterns of thought and see what similar themes appear. What thoughts give you the most energy and excitement? Now look back at your Super North Star and ask yourself: is it actually big and scary enough?

Now that you have your passions and purpose at the forefront of your mind, think about the skills and motives that will help you follow them, and what might stand in your way:

☛ What are your three super-strengths? We are generally drawn to things we are good at, or roles for which we already have skills. Are you actually using your super-strengths in your current role? Does your Super North Star need any other strengths you could develop?

☛ Is anything in life holding you back? We often create a range of excuses to not move forward in the desire to stay safe: it's the wrong time for me; I'm too old to change; I'm not talented enough – and the list can go on. Write down the obstacles in your path and honestly assess whether they are surmountable – or are your own mind and fears getting in your way?

☛ Think ahead to the end of your life's story – what do want to have achieved? What legacy would you like to leave behind for your family and society? What sort of effect do you want to have had on other people's lives? How do you want to be remembered in life? Write those thoughts down.

Finding our Super North Star

Finally, establish how satisfied you are with your purpose; have you identified what it is you really want in life, or do you need to put some more thought into it? Score yourself out of 10 on the questions below, with 10 being perfect. Try not to use the number 7 – that is a safe number that we tend to use when we are hedging our bets.

I am clear on my purpose, it is formulated and comprehensive and I can tell a compelling story about it ☐

I have the necessary skills and desire to get to my purpose ☐

I am energised and passionate about my purpose ☐

I do not allow things to hold me back ☐

I am committed and have already started the journey ☐

I know the legacy I want to leave behind ☐

I manage my time to ensure I focus on the purpose ☐

I have the correct people around me and in my team to reach my purpose ☐

If you scored 0–4 in any area, that is a danger zone and must be improved, as this is a weak area for you and will undermine your performance. If you scored 5–7, there is room for improvement. If you scored 8–10, you're doing well!

Now calculate your overall average and the same rules apply.

The above questions are designed to provoke thought, and to make sure you have confidence in your purpose. They will start to show you your super-strengths as well as the areas that could be holding you back. Where necessary, they will enable you to seek guidance, experience or knowledge to continue to develop the strengths you need and to remove your biggest weaknesses.

Once you have a Super North Star that you are happy with, it's time to work out how you are going to achieve it. But before you embark on your journey, you first need to work out where you are starting from.

Chapter 2

Establishing our starting point

As we begin to dream of what we want to become, or how to get there, we also need to work out where we are, our starting point: what is our potential, what are our strengths and weaknesses, our motivation? And what do we need to work on to help us on our mission? Most of all, we need to recognise that our starting point is not our destination – we have a journey ahead of us, and we shouldn't expect to have all the necessary skills at the outset. One of the greatest inhibitors of achievement is the desire to succeed or be perfect immediately.

The Ancient Greeks knew a thing or two about heroes. For them, heroes were mortal beings who did things so far beyond the scope of normal humans that they were revered, even worshipped after death. But none was the finished article at the beginning of their story; their epic selves were developed and defined by their journeys and their actions. They had to overcome trials and tribulations, failures and defeat, and most had to contend with flaws, such as rage, jealousy, naivety or a weak tendon at the back of the leg. But with each step forwards, and in some cases backwards, they grew in capability, until ultimately they triumphed as heroes.

So if our heroes weren't the finished article when they began their journey, why should we be? We have to honestly

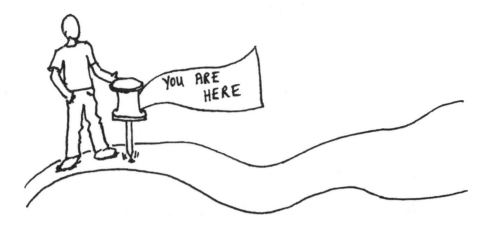

assess how close we are to achieving what we want, and what areas we will need to focus on to improve. What skills we have, for instance, and at what level; the state of our support network and where it might be lacking. From there, we can start planning the milestones we need to reach along the way to achieving our purpose.

'A journey of a thousand miles begins with a single step.'
LAO-TZU

Pushing our potential

Success is not simply bestowed on the lucky few. All of the successful people I have ever met have had to struggle in one way or another to get to their purpose and achieve their dream. First we need to decide how good we want to be and how far we are willing to push our potential to get there.

When I was at secondary school, I was bright and able; academically I could have moved up a stream, maybe two. So why didn't I?

It was actually my teachers who suggested that I stay in a lower stream, telling my parents it was better that I be in the top of a lower group, than the bottom of a higher one. That I might *not* have ended up at the bottom of the higher group wasn't even considered; in fact, the decision to stay put was presented as being the smart choice. I know that had I been moved to the higher group, I would have attained more, because I'm naturally competitive; I can't resist a challenge. But left in the lower group, where success was easy, the consequence was I stopped trying; let a teenage boy coast and he will.

In sports, however, I was the one who decided my goals. I had discovered I was good at a number of sports, and could have played at county level and possibly even higher. In the end, though, I decided I would rather be a good all-rounder than concentrate on just one discipline. I recognised the limits of my potential and knew that if I picked one, although I could compete at a high level, it would never match my dreams of success: Olympic glory, World Cup winner, heavyweight champion. I didn't want to focus on one sport and not be the best at it, so I pushed myself to be good in as many as possible. I ran, jumped and boxed, kicked, hit and threw balls, and practised for hours at a time. And as my dreams began to turn toward the army and the SAS, this was to prove a great advantage in later life (trust your intuition).

We should always make sure we are pushing ourselves to achieve our very best; fulfilling our potential, discovering what we are really capable of, is one of the most important things in our journey through life. We mustn't let other people tell us what we can and can't do, or listen to anyone who does not have high expectations of us.

Find our strengths and weaknesses

To really understand our true potential, we need to determine what our strengths and weaknesses are. Not all of us can be the lead in the film, play or adventure we are on, but we all have unique abilities and skills. Understanding where we shine helps us understand what needs work. For example, it's hard to become an accountant if we're bad at maths – not impossible but more difficult.

'A problem is a chance for you to do your best.'
DUKE ELLINGTON

Although it has taken time to do so, I have identified my strengths and weaknesses through looking closely at my past experiences and honestly assessing where I excelled and where I could improve. I also listened to a number of people who I respect and who have helped me understand myself better.

I now know that I learn best through a hands-on approach, and have good body-kinaesthetic awareness (I am coordinated and in tune with my body); I like physical activity and need an outdoor lifestyle. I have good interpersonal skills, I love understanding and interacting with people. I am empathetic, caring and I want to develop others to reach their potential. I also have good intrapersonal skills – I am aware of my own interests, goals and purpose. I am in tune with my inner feelings; I trust my intuition. I also know that I have a strong will and desire to achieve my goals. I am linguistic and word smart – I am a confident speaker and I can discuss my plans with ease. I have average spatial awareness and I have to work hard to be logical and on my numeracy skills, as reasoning and calculating do not come naturally. I have to work on structure and strategy. I like to think conceptually and explore patterns and relationships. I need to form concepts before I can deal with details. I still need to take more time to plan before jumping straight into the arena. I have also had to learn to prioritise, as I have a tendency to say 'yes' to projects that interest me, even when I have a lot on. I would like to be more musical and learn an instrument (although I have given up on being able to sing).

'If everybody was satisfied with himself, there would be no heroes.'
MARK TWAIN

It's important, of course, to concentrate on our super-strengths as they are key to our success. However, it's also important to make sure that particular weaknesses aren't holding us back and limiting our development. I've found that the best way to deal with these is to identify and try to improve them one weakness at a time – until it is no longer a weakness, and then I look at the next one in line. But I continue to improve all of my super-strengths all the time.

Find our motivation

Knowing our strengths and weaknesses isn't enough to move towards our goal; we have to keep pushing ourselves to succeed, to reach our potential and make sure we're not becoming complacent and, for that, we need to discover what motivates us, what gives us energy.

I vividly remember being on a cross-country run when I was fourteen. It involved all the boys and girls in my year. I had been training hard, as I had just joined a boxing club, and comfortably settled into the middle of the pack, surrounded by my friends. We completed the first lap of four, and I was barely out of breath. But as I passed a teacher I liked, I saw him shrug and turn to a colleague: 'Shame,' he said, 'I thought Floyd would be at the front.'

A burst of irritation saw me increase my speed and, with my friends yelling at me to slow down, I moved through the pack toward the runners at the front. My inner voice coached me onwards: 'Stay with the group, take the next runner, you can do it!' Gradually, over the next two laps, I caught up with the leading group until I was on their shoulders pushing for first. But making up the lost ground had taken its toll. On the final lap, my legs were aching, my lungs were bursting, blood was pounding in my ears, and when they sprinted for the finish line – using reserves I had long since spent – I fell back and finished joint fourth.

But far from being disappointed, I was elated! Even though sick with the exhaustion, I had given it my all and nearly finished first.

All it had taken was someone having higher expectations of me than I had of myself. If I'd pushed myself earlier and run differently, who knows what might have happened. My friends congratulated me afterwards: 'Well done, you were flying, you almost caught Benn.' (Benn was the fastest boy in our year.)

'Next time,' I replied.

Our motivation can come from a number of different places: the desire to help and make a difference in the world; the desire to champion a cause; our own performance, wanting to be the best in a particular arena.

We can influence our own motivation; we just need to learn how and what works for each of us personally.

It's all about staying positive, remembering that we're working towards something. We have to think about what it is we want to achieve, why we want to achieve it and how much we want it. Once we have clear answers to those questions, in moments where we don't feel we want to keep going – if we're struggling to get up early or to finish the last mile of a run – we can return to those answers and focus on them to re-energise ourselves and keep going.

It's important to have set ourselves tough goals, but we need to break them down into small manageable steps, so that we can chart our progress and feel like we're getting somewhere, so we can feel motivated by our success so far. We shouldn't feel overwhelmed by any of our steps – if it feels like there's a lot to do, we should just focus on the here and now, make a start, and we'll soon find that we're well on our way.

Mentors and guides

Although we have a certain amount of control over our own motivation, that doesn't mean that external sources can't help as well – just as my teacher's comment spurred me on in cross-country. Some people need a figure of authority to urge them on, others find it helpful to have the support of other people going through the same challenges. We need to find the people who can help motivate us, whether they are friends, colleagues, a teacher or a trainer, or the like-minded people we meet by joining a group or club.

That's why it's so important to assess our support network right at the start: who are the mentors we have in life? Who can we turn to for honest opinions and advice? Who motivates us, pushes us to succeed and will help keep us on track? Hopefully we'll encounter some of these people while on our journey, but it's helpful to know who is already in our life, the people we can rely on and those who have helped us in the past, to help get us started.

But just as positive experiences and mentors can help shape us, so can the negative ones. What's important is finding a way to remove them from our journey, or turn them into a positive influence in our life, a learning opportunity. They don't have to drag us down.

Initially I left school with only a few qualifications, but passed various exams later in life, eventually being asked if I wanted to undertake a PhD. It was a research project on mental toughness and how the mind works under pressure. I had a very heavy workload at the time, but for some reason I really wanted to take it on still. I took some time to reflect on why exactly I was so determined to do a PhD. To my surprise, I realised the answer was vanity – I wanted to have the title

'Doctor'. And it was all based on the settling of old emotional scores.

When I was eleven, I came top in a maths exam. I was feeling very pleased with myself before Mr Cole pointed out that it wasn't that I'd done well, but that everyone else had done badly, capping the insult with: 'I think we all know Woodrow is far from the cleverest child here.'

Children have a sharp metric of what's fair and what isn't. I knew I had won! I hadn't rigged the game or cheated. It wasn't my fault everyone else did worse. From a factual basis it might have been accurate, but it was hardly encouraging, and the injustice of it stayed with me.

Once I had accepted my reason for wanting to do a PhD, I realised that I did not *need* a doctorate, I just wanted one. Big difference. We can't change what has happened in the past, but we can change the emotional connection to it. I can't change the event that occurred when I was eleven, but I can change the way I think about it, look at the event and smile. I know that the teacher was actually a nice person who reacted without thinking because he was disappointed in the class. As soon as I allow myself to think like this, the negativity associated with the memory disappears and I can move on. We can choose which experiences affect us and how. They can be opportunities to learn and move forward, not live in the past.

Points for action: assessing your starting point

The exercises below should help you think about who you are, and what your strengths and weaknesses are, so that you can evaluate what your starting point is.

Write down as many questions to yourself as you can in twenty minutes, without hesitation and in one sitting (the key is as many as you can). The questions do not have to be significant and should cover any and all areas of life. How can I find work I love? What am I meant to achieve? What is my real talent? How can I be more creative? What is my purpose? If I could be anyone in the world, who would I be? Who's my favourite historical character? Why did I give up the piano? What language do I wish I spoke? How can I be more creative? And so on.

Write your questions, then walk away and come back later to see what they reveal. With this exercise, the questions you ask yourself can be as revealing as your answers. They will show you what areas you are interested in exploring or resonate with you. So don't overthink, just write down what comes to mind. Once you have completed the exercise, take the time to look through the questions you have asked yourself, and what they mean.

Then, write a description of yourself, as the lead character in a story. Write it from the point of view of a friend who knows you well and likes you; they should talk about your strengths and any weaknesses that could hold you back. Take about twenty minutes.

In your description do you see yourself constantly seeking new challenges and opportunities? Are you willing and able to deal with failure? As with any challenge worth taking on, failure is always possible, even likely, to some degree. But doing so simply gives us the chance to learn from our mistakes and do better next time. If we are not failing at some stage, we are not taking enough risks or meeting hard enough challenges. Do you need others to help you pursue your dream? People who achieve success by themselves are the exception rather than the rule.

Do you see a deep sense of meaning and personal identity in your story? When you are passionate about your purpose, it drives you to seek unexpected opportunities and explore uncharted territories, to move forward regardless of the obstacles. Remember, without passion nothing happens.

Now consider the following questions:

- ☛ Do you want to help others?

- ☛ Do you want to develop a product and bring it to the market?

- ☛ Do you want to just be successful in any area?

- ☛ Do you want to be the world's best at something?

- ☛ Do you just want to be safe and financially secure?

☛ Do you want status, e.g. to become the prime minister?

☛ Do you want to help society and leave a legacy?

When I did these exercises, I found I dallied with the first questions, but discovered that the less I thought, the deeper I delved in to my subconscious, and, when I looked back, I discovered amid the jumble two very important themes in my questions and answers: one was the need for personal balance, to be healthy, and the other was a desire to teach and give something back of the things I have learned. The exercise told me it was time to leave the military, set up a business and start thinking about setting up a leadership academy. I could identify a lot of my strengths from my answers, but I could also see the areas that needed work, where my weaknesses would let me down, such as learning about business and becoming more commercially minded.

I AM ...

Establishing our starting point

Write down a list of the key words that define who you are today and the key strengths you have. Spend time doing this and, when you're done, check the list with someone who knows you well, who will support and challenge your list. Do they agree with your chosen traits?

Who are the five most important people/mentors you have had in your life to date and why? What do they think about you?

Write down their strengths and what you have learned from them. Who gave you the most energy? Who gave you the most emotional support? Who gave you the most focus?

If you could pick five people you have never actually met (alive or dead) to guide you on your journey, who would they be and why?

At the end of these exercises you will have a better understanding of the strengths you admire, the strengths you have and the areas you may need to work on during your journey.

I have also found that, when I want to achieve something in particular, it helps to ask simple questions of my mentors:

1. What do you think are my strengths in this area?

2. What do I need to be aware of?

3. What do I need to start doing?

4. What do I need to stop doing?

5. What are my weaknesses in this area?

The grid below allows you to identify the areas you are most competent in. Give yourself a score between 1 and 10 (with 10 being most competent). Then re-score yourself in six months' time. It will enable you identify your weakest areas and to track your progress.

		Date	Date
1	I have great interpersonal skills		
2	I have great intrapersonal skills		
3	I have great linguistic skills		
4	I have great spatial awareness		
5	I have great logic and numeracy skills		
6	I have great body-kinaesthetic awareness		
7	I have great musical awareness		
8	I have great creative awareness		
	TOTAL SCORE		

Chapter 3

Our Ethos

The definition of ethos is the fundamental character or spirit of a culture. It might also be defined as the underlying sentiment that informs the beliefs, customs or practices of a group or society, or the dominant assumptions of a people or period. The word ethics comes from ethos and means the moral principles or ideals that govern our behaviour.

On an individual level, our ethos is the principles or values that we hold dear, that define our approach to life. It is a standard we set ourselves. Our character and the legacy we leave behind are defined by the values we exhibit. At their highest level they are non-negotiable, at their lowest level they are worthless.

'You are not what you think you are. You are what you think.'
THOMAS JEFFERSON

Our ethos develops from our intellect, personality type and traits, from our experiences in life and the people around us, from our understanding of our own moral frailties and the adversities we have experienced. Often built in childhood, it is formed from a mixture of nurture and nature and continues to evolve during our lifetime.

The people who shape our ethos

Mentors can be invaluable – they are people who guide us along our chosen path, who inspire us, shape our values and help us become who we are. They are people whose advice and feedback we can trust.

My mother and father played a hugely important role in my development – they were my first mentors and heavily influenced my early years. I'm sure many of you will have had a similar experience.

My father was a hard-working man whom I respected and loved, and, like all sons, I wanted him to be proud of me. A great storyteller with a warm sense of humour, he loved sports and was physically tough, although never violent – he never even raised his voice to me or my brothers, leaving discipline to Mum.

I remember only one occasion when he stepped in, at the request of my mother, when I was caught stealing penny sweets from the local shop. I knew it was wrong, but temptation and a desire to be part of the gang got the better of me and blinded me to a rather basic fact: the shop owner knew our family. My mother only passed the shop once every two weeks, so I had a fortnight of waiting and worrying about her response. Sure enough, the day finally came. I watched Mum return home clasping her bags of shopping and I knew from her stone-faced ire that she'd been told. I braced myself for the harsh telling-off, denial of treats and enforced early bedtimes. But she simply said 'Wait until your father gets home' and sent me to my room – something she had never done before.

The hours dragged by until Dad returned and I was summoned to the kitchen – alone. The air was one of gloom, and I knew something awful was about to happen. And it did. Instead of shouting or any form of physical punishment, Dad quietly asked me if I felt I wasn't getting enough pocket money. I dropped my head in shame and he told me how disappointed he was in me and that he thought he'd set me a better example. I was despondent. He took me to see the shopkeeper to apologise and penny sweets were safe around me from then on. It was my first taste of emotional intelligence and had a profound effect on how I deal with people who make mistakes. It also helped me to start to define my own ethos. It hurt me to realise I had not had the strength of character to avoid the temptation to steal, or to deal with the peer pressure of the gang which had encouraged me to do so. More importantly, I had let my dad down, and his opinion of me was very important.

That certainly wasn't how he dealt with everyone. Working at the Bradford market, he was a hard man to fool, keeping track of stock and prices in his head, so on one occasion when some crates had been shuffled around and counted twice, with someone pocketing the difference (a basic market fraud), he noticed straight away and his face turned red with fury. Only one man could have done it, and so, after conferring with another director whose face also went red, Dad approached the culprit, grabbed him by the collar, negotiated with him in four-letter words and, lo and behold, five minutes later the missing stock miraculously reappeared, having been 'misplaced' in another van.

'You don't steal from your own,' said Dad. 'There's nothing lower than that.'

I grew to admire my dad for a number of reasons. He was responsible for many of the key experiences that shaped me into the man I am today. In fact, I would say my journey into the adult world really began on the morning of the first day of my first job, with my father's footsteps padding into my bedroom to quietly place a travel alarm clock next to my bed.

It hadn't been easy to convince him to give me the job. Dad was quite protective over us, unlike Mum, who pushed us and encouraged us to take risks. Dad was more conservative. So when I asked him for a Saturday job working alongside him in the market, he refused. I really wanted the job, or, more specifically, I wanted the money a job would bring, because although we wanted for nothing, our family didn't have money for what Mum considered luxuries: football boots, boxing gloves, and clothes a boy might actually want to wear. But I was only twelve years old, and Dad was determined I wouldn't end up in the same tough, cold and relentless environment he'd been in when he was a boy, so he flatly refused.

But I kept asking, and he kept refusing, until one weekend over a lively Sunday lunch when, to my surprise, Mum took my side. She told him I was gangly for my age and physical work might toughen me up and fill me out. My three older brothers took my side too. Under collective pressure, Dad capitulated, albeit reluctantly.

My enormous sense of achievement lasted until the morning of my first day when, having tossed and turned all night, I heard the front door close and Dad leave the house. I glanced at the alarm clock he'd left me: it was 4 a.m. I pulled the warm, soft covers up and fell asleep until the trill of the clock woke me half an hour later. I was about to learn my first lesson in being self-disciplined in order to achieve my purpose: getting out of bed when my brain was firmly telling me to stay put, so that I wouldn't be late on my first day.

Dragging myself out of bed, I questioned the merits of such an early start on a winter Saturday morning, stepped outside into the bitter wind and trudged my way to the bus stop. I caught the bus into Bradford city, anticipation and nerves building. What had I argued myself into?

The bus drove down Manchester Road to the outskirts of the city and, as I arrived at the station at 5.25 a.m., it started to rain. I still had a mile walk to the market. I pulled the hood up of my light Peter Storm jacket and realised why Dad dressed in such warm clothes all the time, clothes that made him look as fat as a bear. At the crest of the hill, the lights of the market glowed warmly against the grey October morning and I could hear the noise building in the valley below. I took in a deep breath and walked down the hill to the entrance of the market.

Bradford market was once fed by cobbled lanes, just wide enough for barrows. It had changed in the seventies into a modern, soulless trading area where trucks had to ease down streets made for horses and carts. Dad had worked for J. W. Swithenbank all of his life, starting as a barrow boy and rising to director of sales. He'd told me that it was either this or the mills. He'd spent one day in the mills and that was enough.

Swithenbank's was first on the right as I walked in, the noise excited yet indistinct, like a football crowd before a kick-off, as vibrantly coloured fruit and vegetables from around the world were hauled in crates by men trading morning conversation with cigarettes clamped between their teeth.

Dad glanced at his watch as I arrived and greeted me with a smile, a silent 'well done'. He handed me a work coat that swamped my frame and set me to work with the men shifting boxes of fruit from one place to another. After a very long two hours, he gave me some money for a bacon sandwich and I made my way to the cafe.

After a quick game of Space Invaders (with a challenge that the highest score each week would win a free breakfast – my type of competition!), my bacon sandwich arrived, and I chomped away, watching deals being struck, wholesalers and traders battling for the best price of the day. I quickly learned that this wasn't like a store – none of the prices were fixed, they fluctuated constantly, reacting to supply, demand, time and quality. It might have been over apples and pears, but if you weren't paying attention you could lose vast amounts of money. The competition was high and status as well as money was at stake.

At 1 p.m. the market finally closed and Dad gave me a lift home. As a Yorkshireman, he didn't tell me he was pleased with me, but I felt his pride like a warm balm and we laughed and talked all the way to the Park Lane pub, where he bought me a half of Tetley bitter (I felt six foot tall) and told me to drink it without being caught or I would pay the fine. Then he told me to go home and tell Mum that he was still doing some business and would be back soon. On arrival, I slumped on the couch to watch TV and woke up a few hours later with aching limbs, pride in my chest and two whole pounds in my pocket.

Yes, the pay was poor and the hours were long and the conditions were tough – freezing in the winter and boiling in the summer – but the men there judged you on your performance and ability, not on who your father was or where you went to school. You gained respect from doing your job well and being reliable and trustworthy. Responsibility was given on merit and performance, regardless of age, and by the time I was sixteen years old I ran cover for the sales department if a salesman was off. Never underestimate the power of acceptance as a form of encouragement. I loved working in the market; it was like a second home.

My time at the market helped me to form my work ethic: hard work, taking pride in what I'm doing, and always being on time. And my dad was a great influence on my attitude, seeing him there every day, the first to arrive and the last to leave – my first mentor, though certainly not my last.

'The happiness of your life depends upon the quality of your thoughts.'
MARCUS AURELIUS

Having positive mentors and role models in our formative years is key, but it's important to have them throughout our journey as we continue to develop our ethos.

Al Slater was my first mentor in the Parachute Regiment. Whether on the battlefield or the sports field, he was the kind of man you'd always want on your side. Highly educated, seemingly taller than his lofty six feet, he had a defiantly square jaw, blue eyes that could see right through you and a robust sense of humour, and he was totally authentic and true to what he believed. He was probably the most influential teacher of his generation, and was looked up to both by recruits and his peers. He continues to shape my thoughts even to this day. He taught me that doing basic drills was neither boring nor a constraint but a liberation. 'If you can do the basics well, it means that you can adapt to a changing situation and release your creativity.' Al's second mantra – 'Never cut corners' – was always said with intent. And we never did, and I never have; cutting corners is the worst kind of false economy. If we're going to do something, we should do it well. It will save us time, energy, and possibly our life and that of others in the future.

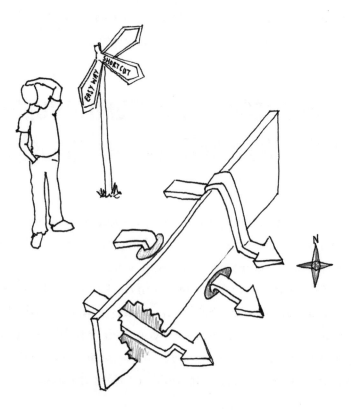

It's a lesson I drill into people now. I once ran a training exercise where I told a group of soldiers to undertake a reconnaissance of an area to prepare an ambush for another night. This always involves detailed planning and execution, and I've found in the past that people often skip steps in training. But bad habits picked up in training can carry over into real scenarios, so it's something to stamp out immediately. What they didn't know was that I had also placed people on the ground to check they did this task correctly and thoroughly. Most of the groups were exemplary but, as usual, there was one group that decided to cut a few corners. The next day I asked each commander to now stand up and explain exactly what steps they had taken – but told them about my men on the ground, so their story had better be true. Seeing someone now have to admit to the choices and mistakes they had made, and how unprofessional they had been, was a lesson for everyone. I also asked that team why they hadn't held the leader to account for being unprofessional. I suspect no one in that room was ever tempted to cut corners again.

Knowing our values

One of my key values is to be courageous, to ensure that I am brave enough to challenge any dark thoughts I may have (the temptation to cut corners is always there) and to call out any colleagues who display unethical behaviour – which can happen even in the best teams.

Our ability to connect what is fair, what is right and what we stand for to the rest of our compass is essential. It requires self-awareness, so that we can demonstrate the characteristics we demand of others. Our ethos becomes our identity or brand: it defines our character, our behaviours, the essence of who we are. How we see ourselves and how others see us is a big driver in our performance – we don't want to let ourselves down, and we don't want to let others down, especially when we are aligned to a set of values and wish to be judged on them.

'Waste no more time arguing about what a good man should be. Be one.'
MARCUS AURELIUS

Our values matter because they influence our behaviour, and so our ethos must be positive to truly reach our potential. If our thoughts are actually about selfishness, jealousy, greed and hate, to name just a few, we do not have a positive ethos, and our approach will limit everything we do in life and eventually catch us out.

What happens when we find a way to easily achieve our Super North Star, but to do so we would have to cheat, lie or break the rules? Would we? Would it be consistent with our ethos?

We could have a set of values that are totally self-serving. Many people do. We can have a purpose, a strategy and a warrior spirit without an ethos, but if we lie, cheat and steal, if we pursue our goals selfishly, without considering the cost to others or society, if we make excuses and blame others, if we stubbornly repeat mistakes or reject advice, we will be found out and we will fail.

I was in a race when a friend of mine grabbed my arm and said he knew of a shortcut through the forest and we could take at least fifteen minutes off our time. Now this was an opportunity to take advantage of better knowledge and get ahead of the competition, but of course the route had been specifically marked on the map, so it would have been cheating. I told him that we should remain on the course. During the race two groups did decide to take alternative routes. They were failed immediately as there were people hidden on the alternative tracks taking names.

Even if we do somehow escape exposure, the one person we can't hide from is ourselves, and we can only delude ourselves for so long. And is that really how we want to live our lives or be remembered? Do we want our achievements tainted in that way? Consider Lance Armstrong, and the effect the doping scandal has had on his legacy. And there are many examples throughout history of people in sport, in finance, in politics, who have lacked a positive ethos; life did not end well for them and history does not remember them kindly.

'The evil that men do lives after them.'
WILLIAM SHAKESPEARE

Sticking to our values

Under pressure, our ethos is one of our foundation stones; when our values are firmly in place, they are unmovable. No matter the adversity, we can resist the temptation to abandon our principles. It ensures that we do not lose sight of what is actually important in life, even if we are presented with an easier path to take, or if it seems that an alternative path is the most practical or even the only option. Ultimately, we are the ones who decide whether we are willing to compromise our values or not, and for that we need courage. With courage, all values are protected; without it, none are.

When I first entered the commercial world, I was presented with ethical decisions I'd never faced in the army. For example, I didn't have a contract with the first company I joined. Our contract was a handshake, with me promising I would remain with them for a year. Not long after, I was approached by an international corporation, offering three times the money, lots of travel and a key role in the organisation.

I was tempted to jump ship – who wouldn't be? And I didn't dismiss the offer out of hand, but resisting temptation is part of the hero's challenge. Does our word mean anything? And if it doesn't, what does that make us? One of my values is giving my word and holding to it – this is about my reputation. It means that I can have a healthy conscience and that anyone who works with me knows that I will always stay true to my word and what we agreed to. So, in the end, despite the lure of money and excitement, it felt wrong, and I turned the job down. We must have characteristics that truly define who we are; values that are non-negotiable and that we are willing to fight for.

I have since had many discussions with company leaders on their ethos. Sadly, some simply use buzz words with no conviction; so when everything is going well they can claim to have high standards, but when things start to go wrong they look for excuses to justify behaving in a completely different way. Their supposed ethos and values have no meaning, when they're so willing to abandon them. That kind of thinking doesn't inspire loyalty or trust. And it doesn't lead from the front.

I was recently involved in a business deal where one of the participants pursued a course of action contrary to the principles he'd previously stated as being core to him. He decided to cancel a contract with someone who had been his friend for over twenty years – it was a contract that had been made on a handshake and up until this time they had never needed a legal document to be in place. He was motivated to do so purely because of his ego and the lure of money. I have seen this man since and he would do anything to change the decision he made, because not only did he lose his friend, he also lost a part of his identity and reputation. His business venture failed and not one of his former colleagues is prepared to work with him. Numerous other opportunities have now been lost to him as people do not trust him; his ethos is fractured and he struggles to look at himself in the mirror. It is, of course, always possible to redeem ourselves after making an error in judgement, and he is trying to do just that, but rebuilding his reputation will be hard work – he has a long road ahead of him.

Team ethos

It is not only individual ethos that is important, but the ethos of any groups that we are part of: a sports team, a company, even a circle of friends. It is important to know that our individual and team values are in alignment. Understanding other people's ethos helps me understand what makes my team members tick, and how we can work together on an agreed set of values. The bedrock of any team is the behaviours we adopt and demand of one another when we are under pressure. It is the essence of who and what we are as a team.

The ethos, the brand and essence of the team, is essential to success. Once this connects with the strategist and warrior, it holds everything together, connects the collective mind and heart and becomes the team's compass. It is particularly helpful when bonding groups that do not have a host of unifying elements but must, nevertheless, come together to perform as one. I recently worked with a high street bank. They had extremely talented individuals in charge of various departments, but did not consider themselves a team because they didn't feel as if they had a common purpose. Of course, the simple fact was that if they did manage to work together, all of them would benefit, including the bank itself. When this was pointed out to them, they were able to come together to align their strategies and improve their working practices as a team, an attitude that has now been adopted by their international departments.

When I joined the SAS, its selection course meant that, without consciously realising it, I was surrounded by people who were similarly steadfast and determined, with high personal standards, because all of these elements had been rigorously tested. This did not stop some of the teams I worked with being difficult and some a dream to work with, but it gave us all several major points of contact to help find a way to work together.

The SAS ethos is clear and non-negotiable. It has stood the test of time for over seventy-five years. We are required to buy into the brand, to become a part of the team ethos, or we are asked to leave. The required standards are:

- The unrelenting pursuit of excellence
- The highest standards of discipline
- The ability to operate in a classless structure
- Humour and humility

The SAS ethos is successful because, once we commit to it, we constantly look to improve our performance and skills; our discipline makes us accountable both as individuals and as a team for the standards we have set; operating without a class structure means we all have a voice and are empowered to lead and take responsibility or to follow when necessary; humility reminds us that everyone counts, whatever their role; and humour gets us through the darkest times and helps us to remember the reason we do the job – because we love it and it makes us smile.

As with personal ethos, it is vital that teams remain focused on their collective ethos, and true to their values. I often work with groups that supposedly have their ethos carved in stone, but, at the first sign of adversity, the behaviours they announce seem to shatter. If we collectively state that integrity is part of our ethos, then we need to be true to that, no matter the situation.

To encourage that, we have consequences when a certain standard of behaviour is not upheld. Consequences are not about punishment; they are about bringing such slips to everyone's attention, first and foremost so that people remember their values and why they are so important.

A positive ethos is important for both individuals and teams when pursuing goals. But before we can make sure we conduct ourselves according to our values, first we need to establish that we know what it is that we stand for.

Points for action: defining your ethos

What elements would you consider as part of your ethos? Do you know what you stand for, what your key values are? Write them down and consider whether someone who knows you would agree if they heard you being described using these values.

Choose between three to five words that you think define your standards of behaviour and that you have demonstrated in the past – for example, integrity. Be clear, with each word, on the behaviour that would be required to show each trait.

Do you consistently conduct yourself according to the words you have chosen? Can you think of any instances where you may not have done so?

Write your chosen words down on your life map. Having them clearly marked down means that every time you look at your life map, you'll be reminded of them and they can help you to decide on a course of action that is consistent with your specified values.

Think about the role models you admire for their ethos and which elements of their ethos you most admire. Which people in your life have had a hand in shaping your ethos and how? Which people do you not admire for their ethos?

Now, from the list below, score yourself out of 10, with 10 being perfect, and remember, try not to use the number 7.

I understand my own motives and I am congruent with those motives

I have humility

I am happy with the person I think I am

I am authentic: what I say, do, feel and think are the same thing

I am consistent: I can be relied upon to always act in accordance with what I say and my values

I always stand up for my ethos when it is challenged

I take responsibility for my own actions

I have empathy for others

My values benefit others

I am aware when I have compromised my ethos

And if you're working within a team, score your organisation's ethos:

My organisation's ethos is in tune with my own beliefs ☐

Our team has a clear code of conduct that is applied consistently ☐

We hold each other accountable for those values and standards of performance ☐

Our team respects and cares for one another ☐

Our team supports each other ☐

Our team communicates effectively with each other and with others ☐

We know each other on a personal level ☐

Our team understands and appreciates the unique capabilities of each member ☐

If you scored 0–4 in any area, that is a danger zone and must be improved, as this is a weak area for you and will undermine your performance. If you scored 5–7, there is room for improvement. If you scored 8–10, you're doing well!

Now calculate your overall average and the same rules apply.

At the end of these exercises you will have a better understanding of your ethos, and that of your team, if applicable. It will show you whether there are any character traits you need to develop on your journey, and whether you think you will be able to stay true to yourself in the face of tough decisions.

————————————————

When faced with decision-making, it's not just your ethos you'll need to keep you on track, but planning and preparation too – which come with developing your strategy.

Chapter 4

The Strategist

The next point on our compass is the Strategist. Having a strategy, along with a plan of action to implement that strategy, is essential to achieving our goals, but it is the element often neglected by warriors.

I myself was once guilty of neglecting this part of my compass. I was twenty-seven years old; I had been a soldier for nine years and in the Special Forces for five. I was sitting in the crew room of the counter-terrorist team when the sergeant major walked in.

'Woody, the adjutant wants to see you, and he wants to see you *now*.'

He looked at me expectantly; I had no idea why I was being summoned, but the sergeant major's tone told me it wasn't a social call.

I ran through all the guilty secrets I thought I'd got away with that year: a fight I was involved in (not my fault, honest); an argument in which I'd upset someone (possibly my fault); borrowing a military boat to go waterskiing on holiday with my family (definitely my fault). So I prepared a number of responses for these contingencies in my mind as I made my way to the adjutant's office.

The adjutant, Jack, was someone I'd known for a long time – in fact he was a friend who I'd competed against, fought alongside, and debated with, sober and drunk. So the formality of the meeting added to my unease. I knocked on his door, was called to enter, and tentatively went in.

'Floyd, sit down.' We made small talk about sport and family as Jack made two coffees, pushed one cup toward me, and then said simply, 'You're being outmanoeuvred, my friend. The ivory tower is concerned: they think you're first rate on a battlefield, in combat or training, but struggling everywhere else.' I stiffened in annoyance and sat up in the chair.

'What do you mean?' I asked, thin-lipped.

'Well, no one can doubt your ability, but you don't negotiate or communicate well, and are far too opinionated. Some are saying you can't see the bigger picture and are dismissive of those you consider don't meet your own high standard.'

I was aware that I was considering how to find out who 'they' were and 'speak' to them, but equally aware that this form of 'negotiating' might not be the best way of proving I could communicate.

'Do you see yourself as a team player?' Jack continued.

'Of course I do,' I said crossly.

'Tell me the team you feel most strongly aligned to?'

I was going to pick my current team, but, seeing Jack's expression, I paused, and suddenly realised I was part of more than one team, and had more than one set of loyalties. What about the Greater Team, those teams that are alongside and in support of me? How aligned was I with the organisation and even my own squadron? Was I part of a wider team or a strategic alliance just coming together for certain projects? I was aligned with certain groups but not others. Why was that, I wondered?

Jack kept the silence going. Then he said, 'Do you think we should be a team and, by that, I mean all of the groups working for this organisation, or something else?'

'We should be a team, in fact we must be a team; it's the only way we can stay ahead of the competition,' I said with relief.

Jack nodded. 'If you can be as good a strategist as you are a warrior, little in the world will stop you. Align those with your core beliefs and you'll be able to drive the change you want to see. Learn to plan and look for alliances; pick the correct battle, not all of them. And think of the greater good.'

My inner voice was cowed into silence. My beliefs were flawed and needed updating.

I nodded and thanked him. 'I know what I need to do. Improve.'

He smiled. 'Now go and do it.'

He looked down at the paper on his desk. My mentoring session was over.

The importance of strategy

Strategy is incredibly important in helping us to achieve our goals. Having a strategy helps us to overcome the odds, much like a chess game where the smallest piece can take the biggest when it is placed in the right position (as Suzanne Hudson taught me when I was ten – I never forget a defeat).

The key to strategy is to ensure we are clear on our purpose and have an adaptable game plan. It helps us to define our short-, medium- and long-term milestones and figure out how to get to them. A milestone may be the winning of a battle or the negotiation of a deal. It might move us towards

developing a business at its highest and most complex level, or towards something like getting fit at its simplest level. Small milestones are just as important as big ones; they keep us moving forwards in difficult times, or when we don't quite know our overall direction yet. And they can make a big challenge more achievable.

Being a true strategist means using our intellect in a logical and objective way, with the minimum amount of emotion and a great deal of patience – anything worth having takes time to achieve. That doesn't mean we shouldn't continue to push ourselves forwards, but we need to recognise success won't happen overnight.

The first step is to ensure we are safe – either as an individual or company (for example, ensuring that we have the correct people around us, are financially secure, have the skills we know we will need). This is what I call 'defending the queen', returning to the chess analogy. Then, and only then, can we look to 'attack the king' (beat the competition, take market share, etc) and achieve our purpose.

Developing our strategic side

Strategy was one of my weakest areas of performance for quite some time. I tended to adopt the warrior mode too easily. I realised this at an early age when discussing an upcoming cricket match with my PE teacher, Mr Tiffany.

'So what is the game plan, Floyd?' said Mr Tiffany. He wanted to know if I had done my homework on the opposition and how I intended to play when I went in to bat. Talking through strategies with him, I had a sudden insight. I needed a game plan for *every* sport, and every time, I played. From that day on, every time I thought about my upcoming performance, I thought about it in terms of a plan. I started training to a plan, I set myself targets and milestones. Each training practice wasn't just a game, it had significance. I started to break down the steps I needed to succeed. I didn't have to be perfect straight away, just aim steady and true towards a goal that was achievable. Once successful, I could realign and move to the next goal.

Unfortunately, despite recognising the importance of strategy, in my youth I wasn't entirely successful in overcoming my warrior mode. Enthusiasm would trump reason, and I would begin most projects with more gusto than thought. This will to achieve meant I often made mistakes but failed to learn from them, and all too often it took longer and I achieved less than if I'd taken the time to think things through first. I hadn't yet realised that talent wasn't enough, that I needed to balance the warrior with the strategist within. Wanting to be perfect on day one delayed my development: I was looking toward the outcome rather than concentrating on performing to the best of my ability and letting the outcome take care of itself.

Later in life, I spent time developing my strategist skills and it helped me enormously. I became calmer, I realised I didn't have to fight every battle, and I communicated more effectively. Of course some people are already brilliant at all this, but perhaps they need to develop their warrior side. Remember, strategy without action is merely theory.

One of my best friends from the intelligence service is a brilliant strategist. He can get to the nub of a problem in moments and develop a plan in minutes. When we discussed this chapter, he was quick to acknowledge that he actually needed to enhance his warrior side. Similar to him is an outstanding CEO I know who runs an international corporation. He was in the midst of an aggressive takeover, which his team did not want. He understood most situations quickly and was able to develop a methodology for success, but he hesitated on this occasion before committing to his plan as he wanted more information. He paused too long and the economic situation changed; he went from a position of strength to weakness. He was still able to salvage the situation and the company, but it turned out to be a much harder struggle than it would have been had he taken action sooner. He learned from the experience, and I have never seen him make this mistake since; but he had to learn to develop his warrior side to become the person he is today.

'Truly successful decision-making relies on a balance between deliberate and instinctive thinking.'

MALCOLM GLADWELL

I experienced a keen test of my strategist skills when I left the military and decided to turn my hand to business. I was no longer a professional soldier who knew his job – and colleagues – inside out. I was a novice businessman who had no idea how novice he really was. I was about to be given some sharp lessons and would need to learn them quickly. Above all, I needed a clear strategy with steps along the way.

It all started off promisingly. The office was large, open plan with wood panelling around the walls. Fresh flowers were put in the windows every day. A large oak table dominated the centre of the room, lit by the glass chandelier above. It smelled clean and official, and was a long way from the army. In the heart of London's Mayfair, one of the four desks was mine. It was my first venture in the commercial world and I was ridiculously excited (as I always am when starting something new), but with a healthy level of apprehension (which is something I've learned along the way). The company I had just become a director of was in the process of acquiring several other companies in the security and technology sector to form a powerful consortium.

We thought having all the key capabilities under one roof – without the need for outsourcing – would both set us apart from the competition and put us ahead of the game. We had excellent financial backing and the future looked bright.

Unfortunately, to succeed, sometimes we need good fortune. Not every day, not all the time, but as Napoleon said of one of his officers: 'I know he's a good general, but is he lucky?' Our company wasn't. Shortly after my first day the financial crisis decided to explode, and almost at a stroke we lost our financial backing as our investors withdrew their credit line. This exposed our company's weaknesses.

The powerful consortium we thought we'd established had not built enough trust, nor established enough confidence in the group as a whole. We had overcommitted in a number of areas and under-researched in others. We had not moved quickly enough to deal with the changing landscape. Only one of the companies we had was making money, but our picture was clouded by too much optimism and not enough preparation, and, in the cold light of day, that optimism was based on promises, which ultimately never came through.

So, I was going to be out of a job; my first foray had resulted in failure.

But at some time or another we will all have to reassess our plans. As German Field Marshal Helmuth von Moltke (the Elder) observed: 'No plan survives contact with the enemy.' We must always be willing to adapt our strategy as circumstances change. I can honestly say I did not (and do not) see this as a complete failure. It taught me to trust my intuition, and highlighted the need for good communication both internally and externally. As long as we learn from our experiences and move forward with that knowledge, we have not failed.

Analysing data

To succeed as a strategist, it is important to properly analyse information to formulate our strategy. We need to consume data, understand it and determine its relevance to our particular situation. And we need to be realistic and free of emotion when doing so, not allowing our feelings to cloud our judgement.

I recently came across a very talented scientist who had changed roles on numerous occasions. At first he had wanted to become a doctor but did not gain the correct grades at A-level, and so became a scientist. While studying for his PhD, however, he realised that all the people around him were actually more talented than he was. He was realistic and accepted that fact, and once again changed tack: he went into media to explain science to the masses and to journalists. He had found his purpose in life, doing something he was good at and loved. That sort of honest appraisal is vital to those who want to succeed in life.

This can be very difficult when, for example, we have built a company from scratch and spent the last twenty years making it one of the most respected in its field. However, when circumstances change unexpectedly, through a shift in the market or new technology perhaps, disciplining ourselves to look at the facts of the situation will help us take the next steps. I have just watched a team that was in this position; the price of oil had dropped to an all-time low, and an improvement in the market over the next year seemed unlikely. Watching them analyse the current market position, their product, their people and their costs without emotion was a perfect example of honest appraisal, especially as they were considering life-changing consequences for themselves and others – their decisions could lead to multiple job losses, leaving people looking for work in an extremely difficult market. They looked at how they could adapt the business for the future; the likelihood of further changes to the landscape; the dangers and risks; what was fact versus what was assumption or prediction. This was all done without anyone trying to protect their own area of responsibility, their ego or indeed their career aspirations. They then had all of the information to hand to make a plan and committed to that plan as a team. I have been fortunate to see this on a number of occasions and it is inspiring to watch a team working together in this way.

'The key to good decision-making is not knowledge. It is understanding.'
MALCOLM GLADWELL

I often see people engage with strategic problems too emotionally. I was once working alongside a businesswoman who fought hard to take over a company in the intelligence sector of a foreign country, because she believed the takeover would enhance her own company. It was an aggressive take-over and it required the clearing out of a number of people in the other company. She succeeded, but, once she'd acquired it, the economic and political situation changed suddenly and the company was no longer going to be a rewarding asset. The best course of action, from a purely practical point of view, was then to sell it. Unfortunately, because she'd fought so hard to win it, she was determined to keep it. She ignored all of the facts, analysis, advice and data because she was too emotionally involved. Eventually she was forced to abandon it, but by that point it was at a great loss and she almost lost both companies.

I have three simple rules when I am given any data.

1. Look at it without emotion.

2. Keep it relevant. If it does not make us faster, stronger, smarter or richer, get rid of it.

3. Keep it simple: don't get overwhelmed by data. If we don't understand it, we shouldn't use it, because nobody else will.

I was recently working with an international sports team who were analysing the data from a recent match. They had access to a wide range of information from the television cameras, the monitors that each player carried and different computer programmes, and they were busy trying to evaluate it all to understand why the opposition had scored against them. They were so busy getting bogged down in an overwhelming quantity of complicated statistics and analysis, it took far too much time to spot the real reason, which should have been simple to spot straight off: five of the seven players in defence all, at the same moment, had their backs turned when the opposition started their attack. So, even though those players were eventually in the correct position to face the attack, they did not have enough time to react and it was too late to defend effectively. If they had simply looked carefully at the information they had easy access to, rather than delving straight into overcomplicated data, they would have saved five hours of needless analysis and the work of three people.

I also have a series of six questions that I ask when considering my strategy and plan of action:

1. What is my purpose, the end goal?

2. What is my ethos and how will that affect my plans and how I behave?

3. What will I need to do, what milestones can I break the end goal into?

4. How will I measure my success?

5. What improvements or changes will I make?

6. What legacy will I leave?

In the military I was once asked to chair a meeting on the future of an infantry unit. I was responsible for looking at the capabilities that were needed now and in the future, but I also had to take into account factors such as the costs and the value of each one. I had to deliver my findings and a plan to the most senior people in that organisation, all of whom were passionate about their area of responsibility, were highly decorated, talented and tough, and were not in a mood to change anything. More than one person told me they were relieved it was not them who had to deliver the message. The mood was tense as we started, as people had arrived with their minds already made up.

But I was confident I knew what to do. I was clear on my purpose: to secure the future of the unit and to ensure it was conducting the most effective training possible for operations in the future, without any bias. I knew that I could hold firm to my ethos, presenting the facts and the difficult decisions to be made honestly and courageously, without fear of offending those of a higher rank, while also being familiar with the values of the organisation. I would have to ensure I kept calm and listened to the points that were raised. I had also prepared myself for the conflict that would occur if I wasn't careful.

I explained what we were there to do and then I broke the session down into milestones. One by one, I wrote all the facts of the current situation on a board: the amount of time we spent training and on operations in each area; the last time a skill or competency was used operationally; the areas we were currently operating in; the numbers of men we had available and the likelihood of getting more; the skills we were lacking; and so on. The good thing about facts is you can't argue against them. I knew I had already partly succeeded, as they realised that something would indeed have to change. They were able to start visualising what the success of the unit could be, realistically, which enabled us to start to analyse what we could change and improve.

This was where I had allowed for changes in my plan. I ensured I listened attentively to any points raised, kept calm and prepared for any conflict that might occur. Together, we identified things the unit hadn't done or needed for over thirty years, so we could then ask ourselves if we still needed that competency or if it could be mothballed.

Soon we were able to agree on a plan of action that could be implemented, knowing full well what legacy we wanted: to adapt the unit so that it could continue to viably operate in an effective way for many years to come. Which we were able to do.

'In preparing for battle I have always found that plans are useless, but planning is indispensable.'
DWIGHT D. EISENHOWER

Information is essential to help us formulate our plan, and planning is the cornerstone of developing our strategy. We can't see the future and we don't know what life may throw

at us, which is why our plans must be adaptable, but we can at least anticipate and prepare for some of the more likely obstacles that may crop up in our journey.

Although a certain amount of planning is essential, there is also a danger of overthinking it. Proponents of overthinking are known as 'shadow strategists'. They are over-analytical; they want more and more information before making a decision. They sit on the fence and try to see both sides of an argument but never fully commit to either. They communicate poorly and do not give clear direction. They keep information to themselves, are not flexible and have unrealistic expectations. They lack the ability to convince others of the plan. Their plans can also lack substance and detail; they do not have contingencies in place. Their ego comes to the fore too often and they disregard the needs of others. They are content to play safe. These people need to enhance their warrior side, and take action. Planning without action will not help us move forward.

Planning for contingencies

There are many things for us to be aware of when planning for contingencies: the political world, the economic climate, our personal health, even the weather. There are many variables in life and wherever possible we need to be prepared for all or some of those things to change en route, and then adapt our plans accordingly. It will never be possible to prepare for every eventuality, but the more we can anticipate hazards, the easier it is to navigate our way through them and the safer our journey becomes.

As in life, military success doesn't just happen. It's both imaginative and methodical. As a soldier I used maps – both physical and mental – to plan every mission. First, I would visualise everything I expected to happen on the planned route. I would start with the drop-off point and what the team would have to do there. I would then imagine the route to the first rendezvous point (RV), the type of terrain and the potential obstacles. I would consider where the enemy might be and what they might be doing, and what the climate and terrain we were to operate on would be like. I would imagine and list all the possible contingencies along the route and how I wanted the team to react if faced with them; for example, by making sure everyone knew the procedures and emergency RV in case the team was split up for any reason.

Only once this mental map was completed would I write the plan down. Then, I would take the team through the journey, breaking each stage down so that everyone knew what was expected of them, questioning them to ensure nothing was missed or misinterpreted. After that we would rehearse the journey during daylight hours and in darkness. We were as prepared as we could be, and able to adapt to whatever happened along the route.

This is a technique that any of us can apply to our strategy: visualising each step and milestone of our journey; accounting for all obstacles and contingencies we can think of; making sure the skills we will need are well practised; and discussing with our team, friends or family to make sure we haven't missed anything, that everyone is heading in the correct direction and knows what their area of responsibility is. I know that many businesses could certainly benefit from this level of planning.

Communication and negotiation

Once we have our plan, communicating it effectively to everyone involved is key. Good strategists communicate well in any medium. Good communication allows us to build foundations of trust and teamwork; to be creative and convey messages that are difficult. Communication is about using our emotional intelligence to build a rapport by connecting at an emotional level, so that the team have confidence in one another. From there comes the ability to influence, persuade and problem-solve together. This is where we can lead without having to assert our authority, which is, in my opinion, the highest form of communication.

Many leaders I've worked with are brilliant strategists. Unfortunately, their communication skills are often lacking. They assume everyone else instinctively understands their ideas, and sometimes completely forget to tell them what their ideas are! I was once in an operations room alongside a chief constable who was running a counter-terrorist operation. I asked him what the current plan was and he gave me a run-through that was superb. I asked him if everyone knew the plan. He looked at me incredulously and said, 'Of course, Floyd – it's obvious, isn't it?' I smiled and said: 'Well, not if you haven't actually briefed them.'

An important part of communication is learning how to negotiate, something on which I received early lessons from my father. He was a sublime dealmaker and, later in life when I was involved in negotiations that could result in life or death, I know that some of the examples he set paid off. Of course, not all negotiations have that much riding on them, but that doesn't mean they're not important lessons, all the same.

One day, my father still had three pallets of strawberries left at 12 p.m. Their morning price, when they were fresh, was long gone, and with an hour to go till closing, they were almost worthless. But spotting a trader going from stall to stall, Dad quickly told me to put 'sold' signs on each of the pallets. I was a little perplexed, but did as I was told.

When the trader came and asked if we had any strawberries, Dad looked full of regret. 'Sorry, Mike,' he said. 'They were all sold this morning.' The trader looked in the back and saw the pallets. 'What about those?' Dad pondered for a moment and looked at his sales book, walked towards the pallets and said almost reluctantly: 'Look, Mike, J. J. Johnston was supposed to pick these up by now. I'll let you have them, but I'll have to charge you the price I took this morning.' Not only did the trader pay the morning price, he thanked

Dad warmly; the best sort of trade – everyone was happy. I saw Dad do this numerous times – he could've sold milk to a cow – and without me even knowing it, he was my first negotiating teacher.

I introduced my children to the art of negotiation when they were young as well. Their mother had told them they couldn't do something and they'd responded with annoyance – a negotiating strategy that, along with whining, pouting and sulking, is one all mothers are utterly immune to.

I quietly told them they needed to build a rapport with her and that only by creating trust and fostering affection could they ever hope to change the minds of others, whether their mother, teachers, friends or, later in life, work colleagues. All three have since used it to great effect and, when finding myself out of pocket or agreeing to something I never intended to, I've often wished I hadn't taught them so well.

My eldest daughter, Rhiannon, once announced the completion of a deal with a smile so broad it bounced into the room before she did. It was her first deal for the communications company she'd just joined, worth over £2.8 million. She was only twenty-five.

As a proud father I wanted to know the ins and outs of the deal, how she had prepared, what had been her strategy, how long it had taken to close the deal, all of which she explained at the same time as revealing what she was going to do with her deal-closing bonus – buy a nice handbag. I then asked her if it was not a good moment to pay me back the money I had lent her for her car. Without missing a beat, she said, 'Daddy, why are you trying to spoil my first big deal? Don't you think I deserve a treat to incentivise me to do even better in the future?' Deal done: Daughter 1, Daddy 0.

My negotiation and communication skills have stood me in good stead through many a tricky situation, where a wrong step could have led to serious consequences.

'He who has learned to disagree without being disagreeable has discovered the most valuable secret of a diplomat.'

ROBERT ESTABROOK

'What do you think will happen today, Floyd?' asked my colleague Rick, as I prepared for one of the most important meetings in my life.

'Who knows,' I said. 'But let's think hopefully. Mind our language. And keep our guns.'

The meeting was with a warlord; I had been tasked with getting him to pull back to the lines of an already agreed peace treaty so that we could begin negotiations for a longer-term treaty. I had a team of eight and we'd been in the country for a month. We'd arrived with very little information, as the speed of our deployment had caught everyone by surprise, but we had managed to contact all the faction leaders bar this one, the most powerful one. To say there was a lot riding on the meeting would be an understatement.

We were also having to work alongside a multinational force. Now, in business the word 'multinational' is often used to mean big and successful. Not so in the military. Not only does it mean multiple languages in play, but also multiple command structures, orders, communication devices (sometimes literally on a different wavelength), politicians and media. If not managed properly, a multinational force can descend into international politics being played for national self-interest. Even when the different forces are operating at their best, they frequently end up at cross purposes with one another.

And the faction leaders knew it. With an absence of clarity and consequences, they'd spent months merrily playing everyone off against one another, with a welter of false promises and false starts. In one case, negotiators had emerged from a meeting believing they'd succeeded, only to discover the vehicles they'd arrived in were now surrounded by landmines; they were literally going nowhere.

And so, tired of retrieving stranded colleagues, we'd decided to start with the biggest man and work down. Being the strongest, if he gave up ground, the others might follow. Unfortunately, although I knew what outcome we needed, I also knew I had no authority or capability to force the issue. There would be no calling in air strikes here. I would need to lead without authority, which requires the highest form of communication.

I'd done as much prep as possible: I knew my purpose and strategy; I'd considered what he wanted and what he needed (not the same thing); and, as plans rarely survive contact with the enemy, I'd prepared for numerous contingencies by role playing with a colleague, with him playing the warlord part with great gusto and frequently hurling abuse at me.

In any negotiations, the more we know about our opponent the better, and these days, with Google, Facebook, Twitter, blogs, etc at our disposal, it's often possible to get an overview of someone very quickly. But not our man (not many warlords blog!), so although we knew what he was capable of, he remained largely an unknown.

I had, however, managed to build something of a rapport with his second in command. A slender man in his thirties, he spoke excellent English and when we shook hands he noticed my knuckles and slightly disjointed fingers and very politely asked me about them. 'War wounds?' he said. 'Boxing,' I said, and he laughed. He told me his commander had been a respected judo fighter before the war. Before long, he'd also revealed the commander had lost a brother in the war and I told him of men I knew who'd been killed in battle. This not only reinforced a sense of common ground, but introduced into the narrative that I and my team weren't diplomats, we were fighting men (which he was sure to report back).

I knew I had to control the dynamics from the start, so was planning to use the basic influencing techniques that I'd learned working with the police, which were developed from the six principles of influence propounded by Robert Cialdini in his book *Influence: Science and Practice*:

1. Keeping our word: as he had agreed to this plan, I would ask him to keep his word.

2. Limited time frame: I would stress the need to seize this opportunity.

3. Offer something: I would flatter him with an invitation to an official dinner in the near future with important people.

4. Soft authority: I would emphasise my team were experts in this field.

5. Common ground: I would encourage him to think of my team as different to previous teams he had dealt with, and more like him and his group.

6. Positive comparisons: I would talk about the power of great leaders, their role in history and the need for them to have integrity, to lead and to create the future.

In other words, it was like a chess game. I was not going to win in the first few moves, but, if I could, I'd make him feel good, noble and hopefully amenable to doing what I wanted him to do.

'Diplomacy is the art of letting someone else have your way.'

DAVID FROST

We walked into the HQ of a white-marble multinational building – a multitude of coalition flags fluttering on the outside – where the meeting was to take place. I left some of the team outside to keep a general eye on things and to warn us over the radio when the warlord and his entourage arrived. I then proceeded to the final checkpoint, where armed police checked our ID cards and let us through.

After crossing the marble lobby, we entered the meeting room, which was luxurious in a corporate sort of way, with paintings along the wall, a long polished table and strategically placed silver trays with bottles of water and glasses along its middle.

From our multinational force there were four commanders from other nations who would also be involved in the meeting, and they were already there, dressed immaculately in pressed uniforms, creased trousers and shiny black boots. And, as some missiles had hit the HQ's outer area the day before, they were all wearing body armour.

I entered wearing dusty clothes, a webbing belt filled with ammunition, rations, water and pieces of equipment, and my weapon slung around my back. And not wearing body armour.

Each of the commanders had his own interpreter, but we had brought no one. From his second in command I'd learned that the warlord spoke English, and I had found in the past that interpreters often smooth over what's said, unwilling to translate things that are blunt, forceful or possibly rude. I didn't want to run the risk of being misrepresented.

The other participants' body language was immediately hostile and I was met with a series of nods, limp handshakes and arms folded (never a good sign). They were not happy that I, the most junior person in the room, was going to be the lead in this meeting. And this was despite the fact I'd temporarily promoted myself from staff sergeant to captain so that they thought they were dealing with an officer. I'd been put in charge by the general in charge of the operation, on the grounds that I had more experience at this type of negotiation than anyone else in the country, so there was nothing they could do about it. That, no doubt, added to their unhappiness.

To mitigate the unease, I began by explaining that we needed a common purpose and clear outcome and that we had just one hour to make a joint plan and give the impression of being aligned. This was met with instant resistance and a babble of 'but what abouts' as they listed their concerns and demands.

I waited for a pause and gently explained that the purpose of the meeting was to establish rapport with the warlord and that it couldn't be rushed. Unless he was convinced we were prepared to see things from his point of view, we would get nowhere.

It didn't work. The babble continued and I was touched on the arm by one of my team, who told me we had fifteen minutes to go.

It was time to trust my instincts or nothing would get done.

I made the room an offer: after I had made the initial introductions and opened the meeting, I would speak to the warlord for about ten to fifteen minutes, after which each commander could present their position to him, without any further interruption from me.

They still weren't happy, but reluctantly agreed, and then set to arguing in what order they should speak to him.

'Why did you do that?' hissed Rick.

'Because I know he's a busy man,' I hissed back. 'The meeting will be over in fifteen minutes.'

Our colleagues called to let us know that he'd arrived early.

I took a deep breath and ran through my checklist: watch my emotions and disguise my displeasure at having to share this meeting; be in the NOW and alert to my opponent's emotions, language and body language; and above all, empathise with the situation he and his people found themselves in, even if I clearly couldn't sympathise with his policies or actions. Sometimes we have to deal with people who have done despicable things; however much we may despise what they have done, we still have to be able to negotiate with them. Again, this is where being able to put our emotions to the side can be invaluable.

'Let us never negotiate out of fear. But let us never fear to negotiate.'
JOHN F. KENNEDY

The warlord and his entourage came into the room and everyone stood to meet him.

The importance of first impressions has become a cliché. But research shows people form 90 per cent of their opinion in the first four minutes. (And, true to form, my impression of the other commanders had been made in half that.) Around three-quarters of that opinion is derived from non-verbal sources, such as appearance. It's important to dress according to what the audience needs. If I'd just been meeting the other commanders, my uniform would have been immaculate and my boots and buttons shinier than theirs. But this occasion demanded something else: a front-line soldier who under-stands what it's like to be at war.

The warlord's eyes slid straight over the others and stopped on me and my team. We were approximately the same build, and I walked towards him and offered my hand. He had a firm handshake and I exerted the same pressure back, keeping my hand straight and maintaining eye contact with a smile. I gave him my name and repeated his, before introducing my team and then the other members in the room. I invited him to sit, pointing to the head of the table. I explained that I was the commander with direct access to the general, who was keen to learn how our meeting went (soft authority). Then one of my team brought in a tray of coffee and I poured him a cup (offer something) and warmly greeted his second in command.

I positioned myself to his side so he had to turn to face me and not the others in the room. I asked him if he would like to tell me what he thought of the current situation and of his main concerns, so that I was fully in the picture. Then I paused and waited. He didn't speak straight away and I resisted the temptation to fill the void. I could sense the frustration building in the room, but still I waited.

When the warlord finally spoke, it was in perfect English: 'Why don't you wear body armour?'

'Because I am a soldier like you,' I said. 'I trust myself to ensure my team and I are able to protect ourselves without it.'

He smiled and nodded his head. 'What do *you* think about the situation here?' he asked.

Trust is a vital component of any negotiation. It requires honesty to flourish and can be quelled by a lie. Even the most difficult of individuals prefer a harsh truth to a soft lie.

'I think the time has come to negotiate peace for your people,' I said. 'No war goes on forever. All soldiers know there comes a time when it stops and reconstruction begins. This always happens, the only unknown is when. For you and your people, I think that time is now. This is where leaders show their true courage, because it is easier to say no.' (Positive comparisons.)

'I have lost my family in this war,' he replied.

'I know,' I said. 'I'm sorry, but I am thinking of those people who could still lose their lives in the future. I am aware you have children, as do I. My second daughter was actually born two days ago and although I am sure she'll never forgive me for missing her birth [she hasn't, and I am reminded that I wasn't there whenever she needs to make a point], I stayed because this peace is a priority to me.'

He paused for a moment and looked down.

'I believe you were a judo player?' I asked. He looked up and smiled. 'A long time ago.'

We continued in this vein as we discussed the merits of each form of unarmed combat (common ground) and I could sense people in the room fidgeting because I wasn't getting to the point.

Eventually, the warlord paused and said: 'What do you need?'

A key element is to know if we have earned the right to ask a question or seize an opportunity that comes our way. I decided I had.

'I need someone to show courage and make the first move. I need a checkpoint to be removed from this position.' I brought out my map and pointed to one of his checkpoints, which was inside another group's territory.

'I can't – it's there to protect you, Floyd,' he said with a smile.

'Thank you,' I said and smiled back. 'But we're more than capable of looking after ourselves.'

He smiled and nodded. 'I will see what I can do.' He spoke into the ear of his second in command, who nodded. I thanked him for his time and asked if we could meet again, possibly for lunch or dinner (again, offering something), and he said that he would like that. I knew it was time to close my part in this meeting and opened up the conversation to the others. As I did, the warlord said: 'My apologies, I have been told there has been an incursion and I need to leave. My second in command will stay and discuss your concerns.'

We left the meeting and, twelve hours later, watched the checkpoint being dismantled and the concrete blocks broken up, which then allowed me to go to other factions and ask them to do the same (keeping our word).

Negotiations are rarely a single event – most involve a long-term relationship. I have been involved with many different types of negotiation and every time I had to be aware of the other person's perspective in order to create a connection with them. Without rapport, there is no understanding, and without understanding there is no common ground and there is no room for compromise. The same applies when trying to connect anyone to our purpose. We must do so on an emotional level, building rapport and trust.

But effective communication is just one part of becoming a successful strategist. Working out exactly where our strengths lie and what we need to improve are the first steps.

Points for action:
Developing your strategic side

Do you exhibit the key characteristics of a strategist? Score yourself out of 10, with 10 being perfect. As before, try to avoid using the number 7.

I find it easy to identify the facts of a situation ☐

I can take complex problems and simplify them ☐

I don't over-analyse information and can get to the nub of a problem quickly ☐

I am able to prioritise effectively ☐

I can be flexible in my strategy ☐

I always think about contingencies ☐

I can communicate my strategy clearly to all those who need to know about and implement it ☐

I am realistic about my abilities and those of my team ☐

I am realistic in understanding whether the purpose is achievable ☐

I am patient in my endeavours to reach my purpose ☐

I ensure I make decisions in an appropriate time frame, so I do not procrastinate ☐

I am able to set aside my emotions to look at a problem calmly and rationally ☐

I am able to look at a situation without my ego interfering ☐

I can listen to and consider advice or opinions that I may not agree with ☐

Now consider how well you are able to negotiate and communicate. Role playing with friends or colleagues can be an invaluable way to practise this and see where your weaknesses lie, but first assess yourself:

I listen attentively to people in order to understand their position, whatever my thoughts may be ☐

I am able to bring together people with different viewpoints or goals in order to achieve a common purpose ☐

I can put across my position effectively to all audiences ☐

The Strategist

I am aware of the effect my body language has on an audience ☐

I know the importance of the first impression, and know how to create the appropriate impression ☐

I am aware of others' body language and can understand what that means ☐

I can build rapport with people quickly ☐

I can establish levels of trust with people quickly ☐

I can ask open questions in order to gain more information ☐

I regularly engage in role play to practise difficult negotiations ☐

I put in as much preparation as possible, on the situation and the other participants, prior to opening negotiations ☐

I am skilled at responding effectively to unanticipated questions or scenarios ☐

I am skilled at influencing and persuading others ☐

I am able to find effective compromises that benefit all parties ☐

If you scored 0–4 in any area, that is a danger zone and must be improved, as this is a weak area for you and will undermine your performance. If you scored 5–7, there is room for improvement. If you scored 8–10, you're doing well!

Now calculate your overall average and the same rules apply.

Once you have established your strengths and weaknesses as a strategist, you can see where you need to improve. And you are ready to start developing your strategy to achieve your Super North Star.

Only you can devise your strategy, but one of the most useful things you can do is to break up your goal into small milestones. Think about all the things you may need to achieve before you can reach your final destination. You can make your milestones as small as you like – the key is to make sure that you are hitting them, that you feel like you are moving forwards and achieving something. Give yourself targets, dates to have accomplished certain steps by. Consider what obstacles might arise, and how you will adapt your plan in those cases.

Draw all of these things on to your life map – this is where it really starts to come alive.

———————————

With your strategy in place, it's time to find the strength and courage to put your plan into action – to find your Warrior Spirit!

Chapter 5

The Warrior

The warrior is the final point on our Compass for Life. The warrior is within all of us. It is in our inherent ability to fight for what we want and believe in. It is the aspect of our compass that involves taking action, and delivering on our goals.

Now, I don't want us to be hung up on the term warrior. A warrior is not just someone who has been to war. It's not just about physical strength either. It is about strength of character. We see the warrior spirit in children when they stand up to the bully for the first time or, when knocked down, dust themselves off and begin again.

I've always been fascinated by the brave. I remember listening to my father and grandfather – both boxers before me – spending evenings together trading stories of their time in the ring. Uproarious and often funny, they talked not only of victories, but defeats too. Sometimes they talked of a horrible battering, or a lucky punch, or even the occasional low blow. I was in awe that they bore no grudges and, no matter what, always stepped back into the ring.

So it's no surprise that I was drawn to fighters.

Physical strength and a fighting spirit are, of course, not the be-all and end-all in the warrior approach, but physical health is certainly an important part.

'Warriors are not what you think of as warriors. The warrior is not someone who fights, because no man has the right to take another man's life. The warrior, for us, is the one who sacrifices himself for the good of others. His task is to take care of the elderly, the defenceless, those who can't provide for themselves, and, above all, the children, the future of humanity.'

SITTING BULL

Health and well-being

Fitness is a fundamental discipline. Not just from the obvious point of being fit and healthy to do the job but because when we are fit and healthy we think more effectively and make better decisions for longer periods of time – especially when under pressure. It's not about physical perfection, it's about our personal well-being and making sure we are in tune with our bodies: if we don't take care to eat correctly, and to rest and recharge, where will we get our energy from? I am certainly at my best when I have taken time to keep fit, eat a healthy diet, have fun, rest, take a holiday, and spend time with family and friends. I always like to maintain:

- My general fitness
- A healthy balanced diet
- An appropriate amount of sleep, rest and recovery
- A positive and calm mentality
- A balanced lifestyle

Throughout my life I have tried to look after three areas of fitness: my aerobic ability, strength and flexibility. In theory, to be aerobically fit we only need to train three times a week for thirty minutes, including a warm-up and warm-down. If combined with strength and flexibility, the effects on the mind and body are significant.

The benefits of being aerobically fit mean that we can think more effectively for a longer period of time and have more energy. With aerobic fitness, our brain is the prime beneficiary because it uses as much as 40 to 50 per cent of all the oxygen we inhale, but also our muscles become leaner and stronger and we tend to sleep much better. At the same time, thirty minutes of quality strength training three times a week working through different body parts will help build our core muscle to ensure that we minimise injury and assist our body to operate at a higher level of performance.

I have always done well in the strength and aerobic areas, but I have sometimes neglected my flexibility. This is a mistake as the benefits are substantial. One of the most important elements of training for me is the ability of my joints to move freely, and because of a number of injuries I have sustained during my life, this has become more important to me as I have gotten older. I have just gone back to an intensive programme of flexibility and I am in less pain, my body moves more freely and I feel much healthier. Flexible muscles help prevent injury; stretching our body in the morning, prior to exercise, and in the evening is one of the best ways to do this and should be done on a daily basis. Exercises such as dance, yoga and Pilates are ideal.

If the three elements of aerobic fitness, flexibility and strength are in place, our energy levels will be significantly improved, as will our well-being. The mind and body are not separate, they are connected and need to be in harmony for us to perform at our best.

With a busy lifestyle we can make many excuses for not eating correctly. But if you think you make great decisions at five in the afternoon after eating half a sandwich and drinking ten cups of coffee, you are wrong. We need to eat a diet with as much fresh food as we can. Our mind and body need vitamins, minerals and nutrients to function at an optimum level. We should vary the times we eat at and learn to say no to eating just because we are bored. I travel a lot and have to use a lot of discipline not to take the easy option (and, yes, of course I sometimes do take the easy option, but I always feel guilty and try harder the next time). Being in tune with our bodies is very important; if we sit still for a moment and allow ourselves to think and be mindful of the situation, we will know what to eat and what to say no to.

I love to take time out during the day to rest. This can be a simple twenty minutes of meditation. It allows me to declutter the many thoughts I have and focus on the most important ones. Sleep is also one of the best forms of rest and recovery. It enables the brain to integrate the day's experience by filing and sorting information. Having an appropriate amount of sleep (about eight hours) is important to the recovery of our minds and bodies.

Our own attitude to our health, then, is an important factor in the quality of our lives. A negative mentality can have a major effect on our health, causing increased blood pressure and stress, to name just two adverse elements. A positive mental attitude has the direct opposite effect, increasing our testosterone and minimising our cortisol levels.

Maintaining a basic level of fitness and health is an important part of the warrior spirit, and it helps us to focus on the activity we are currently engaged in. Much is made of advanced skills and training, but actually, one of the most important things is to practise our basic skills, so that they become second nature. In many ways, they will lay the foundations for our warrior approach to life.

Get the basics right

With our basic skills in place, whatever they may be, we improve our chances of success. Such concrete foundations give us an excellent base to work from. It means we can act on instinct when required to do so under pressure, adapt our plans more easily, and come up with creative solutions when faced with a challenging situation.

'We are what we repeatedly do. Excellence, then, is not an act, but a habit.'

ARISTOTLE

On one mission I was part of, we were moving through the countryside en route to an ambush position. We were behind enemy lines and there were over thirty of us, each tasked with a part of the mission. There were those in the main group, those in the cut-offs, and the rest in key positions as a contingency. It was pitch black, cold and wet. We arrived at the drop-off in a helicopter; as soon as it landed we moved to all-round defence and, after it left, we watched and waited for ten minutes to ensure we were alone. It took us two days to reach our final destination. We moved through each of the checkpoints with ease. Nothing was said; no words were needed – everyone knew what they were supposed to do. Each person covered their arcs of fire as we moved across the terrain. We stayed overnight in one location and the next night we closed in on the target area. As we moved towards the final rendezvous, the enemy arrived both earlier than expected and from an unexpected direction. But it didn't matter; we had prepared for this contingency. A series of simple hand signals pointed out the new direction of the enemy and everyone moved into their new positions, quickly and without fuss. The leader was too far away to take control, so another commander made the decision to attack. Within moments the terrorists were arrested. It had gone as smoothly as a drill. The circumstances had changed, but we simply adapted our plan. Basic skills practised beforehand, no cut corners, and everyone knew their role.

'Advanced training is the basic things done exceptionally well.'
AL SLATER

Doing the basics well has stood me in good stead my whole life. People often think the supremely talented have some rare and magical quality, whereas everything I have witnessed, in whatever field, has affirmed to me that the most talented individuals excel at the simple things, the basic requirements of their job. They practise them to death until they are so engrained in their psyche that even under extreme pressure they do not falter.

Practise, practise, practise

Warriors dedicate as much time as possible to honing their skills. When I was younger, I spent hours and hours practising a variety of sports. As long as there was a ball to hit, a time to beat or a glove to thump with, I was happy. I felt free and found I could focus for longer and longer without needing a break, so that once I'd learned a skill, I could test it repeatedly before I even had to compete. Once I started doing that, it stopped being about winning and just became about how good I could be. I'd challenge myself to hit ten perfect shots before I could leave the court. To beat my last sprint time.

To do more squats. And I discovered that the more pressure I applied, the better I performed.

I grew to love the adrenaline coursing through my body and my heart rate increasing, and the doubts that sometimes creep into a tired mind were easier to dismiss or negate. Most importantly, I started to like the nerves I felt before I competed.

Practice is key to improving our skills, and with skills comes confidence, but patience is also an essential part of it. Most skills take years to perfect. Being able to wait, and invest time in ourselves, especially in a world of instant gratification, is more important than ever. Patience is a virtue because things worth having take time to achieve. *Carpe diem* is all very well, but we cannot seize map-reading, any more than we can seize piano playing. Those who are prepared to practise, practise, practise are the ones able to perform on any day.

'What I hear, I forget. What I see, I remember. What I do, I understand.'

CONFUCIUS

Before I step into a pressure zone, I make sure I am fully prepared. This means I have done my research on the relevant people and/or the situation I have to work in, that I have the appropriate skill levels or find them from elsewhere, and that I have practised everything I need to do with the appropriate contingencies in place. This will involve role-playing to make it as real and as difficult as possible.

During training in the military we use actors that have limbs missing to play the part of casualties and civilians – with professional make-up artists creating the mass of blood you would find if someone really lost a limb. It can be disconcerting and I have seen soldiers faint because of the reality of the training. But it means that when you come across a genuine battlefield casualty, screaming because they've lost legs or arms, you can respond appropriately – which is to treat them without fainting.

I was once asked to train an East European Special Forces group. I spent two days watching them shooting on the range and undertaking a number of physical tests, at which they were excellent. I then watched them storm a building, which they did with aplomb. But I noticed the building they'd stormed was conveniently empty, with no doors and no furniture, and in no way resembled a building they'd have to fight in, were it for real. I asked if I could run their next training programme in two days' time, which, being pleased with themselves and confident in their ability, they agreed to. I then took their quartermaster aside. Having secured his secrecy, we drove a truck to their storeroom, loaded it with furniture and office equipment that we then distributed throughout the building, blocking doorways and barricading entrances. It was exhausting, but when we'd finished, the quartermaster laughed and said in broken English: 'This will be interesting, they've never trained like this before.'

The next day, the teams turned up bright and early, anticipating another storming success. I asked them if they were ready. 'Yes, sir!' they said in unison. I lined them up, put people in position as if for a real assault, and told them that they had to conduct an emergency attack, as we had limited information. I asked them if they understood. 'Yes, sir!' I told them to attack. As soon as it started, it went wrong. They struggled to get through the first door (which we'd bolted *and* nailed shut), they fell over furniture, they forgot their drills, and, more than once, they were lucky not to have shot each other, as they were using live ammunition. When eventually they finished, they were furious with themselves, and even more so with me. They were here to be trained, not tricked! I simply asked them if the terrorists in their country were helpful enough to empty their buildings of all furniture, open every door and stand in specific positions when attacked? They burst out laughing. I was forgiven and they learned a valuable lesson. Later I taught them adaptive techniques that would enable them to succeed whatever the situation or threat, and the group seized this opportunity to grow. They went on to become one of the most talented foreign armies I ever worked with.

Pressure training

Training people under pressure, with consequences for those who fail, motivates them to perform to the best of their ability. I work with a lot of children and when I started I was sometimes told, 'We take the pressure away from the children.' I asked, 'Why on earth would you do such a thing? Surely it is better to teach a child to deal with pressure in a safe environment so that they are better prepared for the pressure that is most definitely coming their way if they want to push their potential?'

Of course we have to protect children, but I'm certain that the more challenges and excitement they're exposed to, and the more they have to overcome, the more they'll achieve in later life. I used to build an assault course for my kids every time we went to the gym; I'd go off and train while they ran around jumping over obstacles, balancing on beams, climbing ropes and doing exercises. Over time, I made it more difficult, dangerous and challenging and they kept pushing themselves further and further. To this day they're all excellent at climbing and, just as importantly, taking on challenges – to the point where they'll now challenge me (far too often) with: 'You're not scared to do this are you, Dad?'

So I'm a firm believer in tough targets and pressure training. When I work with sports teams, those who fail to make a set target have a penalty task to perform as a consequence. Creating consequences like this makes the target mean something. It pressurises our physiological responses as if we were performing for real. One of my favourites is the 'five-minute test'. This is five minutes of exercise; a minute each of press-ups, sit-ups, burpees, star jumps and squat thrusts, with the added incentive of being watched by those who didn't fail. The test is brutal and it's rare someone doesn't feel ill afterwards, but as a motivational tool it can't be bettered.

The same idea can be applied when I'm running a business programme: if the participants don't perform well in an exercise, I run it again, only this time I make it longer and more complicated, changing people's roles and responsibilities so that everyone is doubly challenged. I've learned that once teams get used to pressure training, they develop an immunity to the stress and actively seek harder and harder tests in order to keep improving. What's more important is that they also start to enjoy it.

Pressure training with consequences ensures our decision making is at its most effective. Consequences engage the reptilian part of our brain – the part designed to protect us – and, once trained, it can see problems as challenges rather than sources of fear. We perform at our best, think quickest and move fastest when operating in the space between chaos and calm, when we are 'in flow'.

Once people are consistently performing well under pressure, they can be put into ever more difficult situations with more complicated scenarios and distractions. The step up encourages them to really think on their feet and trust themselves to adapt. If the training can be at least as hard as the real event, people will be prepared for almost anything.

Stay disciplined

A key part of all this training and practising is discipline; without it, it's easy to give up. It takes real discipline to get out of bed on Christmas day to go training in the cold and wet when everyone else is watching us through the window; to manage our time effectively; to stay focused on the task at hand; to stick to our ethos and performance standards; to maintain our physical fitness; to keep learning and enhancing our wisdom.

In sport, poor discipline is easy to spot: if a player is sent off, or put in a sin bin, it can cost the team the match. If a top player is banned for many matches, the whole season can be placed in jeopardy. In the military, if an enemy breaks through a defensive position because of a lazy sentry, or an ill-disciplined response, the consequences can be fatal. In business, poor discipline can eventually lead to the collapse of the entire company.

Discipline helps us to perform consistently to a high standard. What helps us to maintain our discipline, more than physical strength, is mental strength.

Training our mind

We all have an inner voice. In fact, most of us have more than one; a confident one, a fearful one, a boastful one. Some have an entire radio set in there. In order to succeed, we need to train our minds the same way we train any other skill, ensuring we only listen to our positive voice, the one that's telling us to push on, to ignore discomfort, to ignore any fear and nerves – and never give up. And that requires practice. It requires us to put ourselves under pressure and to do that as often as we can so it just becomes part of our normal behaviour.

Having control over our inner voice can help us push through to succeed. We can learn to overcome our negative thoughts. That is not always easy to do at first, as I discovered when I was younger. I went to an old Victorian church primary school, with an old Victorian-style head teacher, Mr Edison, whose strict standards of discipline I was able to outmanoeuvre by being good at sports. When I was eight, I was entered for my gold-standard swimming test.

The first test involved jumping fully dressed into the deep end. Not a natural state of affairs for a swimming pool, but necessary for surviving a shipwreck or jumping into water to save someone, which inspired me, even if it was an unlikely eventuality for an eight-year-old. I could imagine myself leaping into canals, rescuing people, and feeling heroic. Plus the badge had the word 'gold' on it and I wanted it more than anything. And Mum would approve.

Only two of us had made the cut. I was a slight boy, and I was clearly nervous. The other, older boy looked quietly confident.

We jumped in and, as the water closed over my head, I realised I'd made a horrible mistake. The sodden clothes dragged me down and, instead of treading water like a hero, I started to choke like the one needing rescue, flapping my arms wildly like a wounded duck, convinced I was going to drown, no, that I *was* drowning. The harder I tried, the worse it became.

The voice inside my head was panicking: 'Don't die, get to the edge. NOW!'

The problem was, if I touched the side I failed. Meanwhile, the other boy was succeeding effortlessly and looking rather smug.

'Floyd!' boomed Mr Edison, his voice overriding the splashing and my inner voice. 'You've done this before, boy! Get your legs working together, bring in your arms, stabilise yourself!'

Even at eight I was good at following orders, and his voice helped me to regain control over my mind. Within moments I'd calmed down and settled into a rhythm, treading water and breathing steadily, definitely not drowning. I wasn't beaten. And I got my gold badge.

On that occasion, I'd needed an external source to help me get my inner voice under control. These days, I have what I call 'internal power words': words or phrases that can inspire and focus us in difficult times. One of my important internal power words is 'courage'. I will often say 'You need to be courageous today, Floyd', and that alone can give me a powerful surge of energy, belief and confidence. Having a positive internal voice is essential, and our power words help to reinforce this.

'Remember when life's path is steep, keep your mind even.'
HORACE

Pushing our performance

Whenever I train people, I can generally spot when they are about to give up. It's in their body language. Do they stand tall and exude confidence? Do they look focused or fearful? Do I see low energy levels or that look in their eyes of determination to succeed? When I hear them speak to themselves or others, do I hear belief in their voice or hear them prepare to fail, saying how tired they are, how difficult the conditions are, how they have too many aches and pains to continue, how unfair it is? I love showing people that with a little more self-control and belief, they can push themselves physically even further than they thought.

I recently saw an international team go through a tough physical fitness test prior to a big match. It was a cold day, there was a slight headwind and I watched their body language and listened to their self-talk: 'We shouldn't be doing this now'; 'The wind is too strong'; 'My personal best's good enough'; 'I have a slight niggle'. I instantly knew it was not going well. Only one man beat his personal best (proving it could be done), but most didn't come close. They'd individually and collectively decided to fail before they'd started, and had even worked out why they were going to fail and why it wasn't their fault.

And they'd done all this, if not at a conscious level, then most definitely at a subconscious one. When they'd finished, I asked them if they had pushed themselves to the limit. One of the players raised his arm and said he could physically do no more. I asked them if they'd pushed themselves to their limit mentally?

And the rest was silence.

On another occasion, I was visiting an international arena with my daughter. I love sports grounds! I'm flooded with the same sense of excitement I got before a deployment: the heightened awareness, the energy pulsing through the group, each person mentally preparing for what comes next. It always gives me a thrill.

On this occasion, I was just there to see the team doctor – my knees don't have any cartilage left after a lifetime of carrying rucksacks and weapons and doing too much sport, so every six months they have to be injected with a steroid and a lubricant to lessen the pain and enable me to walk.

While there, I overheard a meeting discussing the team's fitness and their various programmes to deal with it (I wasn't trying to listen in, but it couldn't be helped and, anyway, team fitness is my kind of gossip). I thought I was being discreet but, apparently, my irritation and agitation showed, because later that day two of the people from the meeting came to find me, looking rather sheepish.

They'd seen me leave and asked me if I'd heard their discussions and did I have any thoughts? I considered whether they really wanted to know, and decided to tell them anyway.

'It sounded like you were planning on making the physical tests easier, because some of the team are struggling,' I said. I paused a moment to see if I was right. No reply came, so I continued: 'Instead of training hard as a team, you were considering putting the failing members on individual programmes, so they didn't look bad or feel singled out?'

There was still no disagreement, so again I continued: 'Now, if that was because of injuries or age, that's one thing. But you and I know it's because they're not willing to push themselves. That's the difference between wanting an international career and wanting to be number one in the world.' I was on a roll, so I pointed to my fifteen-year-old daughter Rosie: 'She could pass the tests you were planning, and if she couldn't, we would have a long, hard discussion.'

My point was made; they decided not to ease up on the tests.

If we want to be the best in anything, there is always a price to pay. It just depends on whether we are willing to pay that price.

'Mastering others is strength. Mastering yourself is true power.'
LAO-TZU

Using our intuition

The objective of training is to get our mind and body into the perfect performance state, by ensuring we have the skills to perform under pressure. Using and controlling our mind is an essential part of being elite. Once we have both physical and mental strength, it allows us to access something that is key to the warrior: intuition.

Intuition is the result of practising our skills so they are embedded in our subconscious, so that in any situation we instinctively know what to do without having to waste valuable time considering how to act. I often ask people to sit down and take in a few deep breaths while they clear their minds. I then tell them I am going to ask them a difficult question, but that I want them to tell me the first thing that comes into their minds. Once I ask the question, inevitably they give me the answer they know is best for this situation. Whether they act upon it is another matter.

Warriors don't stand still wondering what they should do; they make decisions and find solutions. They're calm and cool under pressure. When I am in warrior mode I've mentally rehearsed every conceivable contingency and I trust myself to make the right decision. People who doubt themselves usually do not have the appropriate skill levels, or have not placed themselves in the pressure zone enough.

A warrior's intuition comes from the wealth of possibilities they've built up in their minds by repeated practice. I've been asked on numerous occasions after an event why I did one thing rather than another. I could only answer that it was because I knew it was the correct thing to do, that I hadn't even had to think about it.

Warriors must be alert to changes in the environment, in

people, in politics. Their finely tuned antennae allow them to be ahead of the game, to save time, because they have anticipated things before the competition. I've noticed the most successful leaders in the military, sports or business fields can look at a complicated situation and understand the contingencies they need before action takes place; their intuition comes alive and they adapt without a second thought.

'Strength does not come from physical capacity. It comes from an indomitable will.'
MAHATMA GANDHI

I've been fortunate to see warriors in many different guises. When working as the head of a counter-terrorism team, I was told about a young woman police officer. She had only been on the force a few years and was teamed with an older officer nearing retirement. Out on patrol, she observed a young man taking photographs, which is not unusual in central London. However, there was something about him that seemed out of place. She couldn't put her finger on it, but it didn't feel right. She told her colleague about her concern, but he dismissed it, keen to get back to the station and finish their shift. Approaching clocking-off time, the last thing he wanted was all the paperwork that went with an arrest. But the young woman wouldn't let it go. She approached the man, asked him a few questions and found his answers needlessly evasive, which fuelled her suspicions. Without the older officer's consent, she decided to arrest him under the

Terrorism Act. That arrest eventually led to the capture of a terrorist cell, who were in the midst of planning an attack of untold carnage in the City of London.

The warrior part of my make-up keeps me safe; it's on the lookout for threats at all times and can't be turned off. It is my perfect friend because it ensures I'm at my best when I am in the zone, so I know when to fight, when to withdraw and when to defend. I can operate at a tactical, operational or strategic level as required because I know when I need to be a leader and when a follower. My warrior mode enhances my competitive, courageous side; it helps me build teams because my willingness to fight for what I believe in sets an example for others and inspires them; and, crucially, it enables me to survive.

Accept failure and learn from it

However hard we strive for greatness, practise, train and improve our physical and mental strengths, there will be times when we don't come out on top. Failure is a part of life; not everyone can succeed. The things that matter are making sure that we have done our best; that we learn from our mistakes; and that we refuse to give up. We mustn't fall into the trap of wanting to be perfect on the first session or be disappointed because someone picks up a skill more quickly than we do. The warrior simply continues to practise and practise, until eventually they succeed.

In this, I had a particularly lucky start in life, being born to a mother who wouldn't let me win at cards. Or tiddlywinks. Or anything. A no-nonsense northern egalitarian woman – my mum wouldn't have let the Queen win – she did it without malice, crushing me in a good cause. She explained that there was a mentality to success: 'You're too emotional, Floyd,' she'd say. 'You try too hard – relax and play your best game.' Once we started playing, despite my father's entreaties ('Let him win, just once.' 'No.'), the gloves were off. You either won or you didn't, even if that meant losing some of your pocket money (or, more frequently, all of your pocket money). Otherwise you'd never learn to do better next time, because, as she taught me, as long as you don't give up, there's always a next time. And she took the time to teach me *how* to play and, although passionate about winning herself, always wanted me to do well. The only regret she would allow me was if I hadn't tried my best.

From her I learned that losing is educative, that consequences keep us focused and, above all, that trying our best gives us the greatest chance of success. There is nothing to fear from not succeeding, only from not giving something our very all. It taught me to approach life with passion in everything I do.

I still don't like losing to this day, but if I know I've tried my best, it softens the blow enormously.

Likewise, many years later, I had my first boxing match as a junior. Despite my work at the market, I was still a tall, skinny boy with long arms and legs and, to my despair, I lost on points to a quicker and better boxer. I felt I'd let myself and everyone else down, but, on the way home, Dad consoled me over a bag of fish and chips. 'Even the very best lose sometimes,' he said. 'There'll always be critics but the person in the ring is the only one that matters, and it's important how they dust themselves down and get back up. It is how you deal with adversity that will determine your success. I'll judge you on what you learn from this and no more.'

'Only a man who knows what it is like to be defeated can reach down to the bottom of his soul and come up with the extra ounce of power it takes to win.'

MUHAMMAD ALI

Never give up

Getting back up is key: as my instructors in the Paras explained to me, in no uncertain terms, Parachute Regiment soldiers do not 'jack' – EVER. This attitude was drilled into everyone, every day, until it became ingrained as an internal mantra.

I teach a similar mentality when working with sports teams, like the under-19 England Cricket Team. On one battle run through miserable muddy conditions, one of the players was struggling to keep up and his nose started bleeding and showered down his white T-shirt, but we still had miles to go. I suggested he return to the training centre, but he shook his head. 'I'm not stopping,' he gasped. 'I'm not letting anyone down.' And he didn't – although I had some explaining to do when we walked back into the training centre.

Having a strong warrior approach has helped me achieve things many people doubted I could. When I applied to the Special Air Service (SAS), I was twenty-two, the youngest on the course and, despite four years in the Paras, neither the fittest nor the most experienced. The course itself is legendarily tough and considered one of, if not the hardest in the world. It's run twice a year; during winter when it's bitterly cold, with snow and ice on the ground, which slows the metabolism and can cause mental confusion (cold slows our thinking), and during summer when the heat can be debilitating and the extreme physical exertion can cause dehydration and fatigue. Few make the grade, and that's the intention. The selection staff are highly experienced at spotting those mentally and physically resilient candidates, with integrity and self-sufficiency and the ability to work in a team. And a sense of humour is not a bonus, it's a must.

All those on the course are volunteers and come from all three services, including the reserves. Today, soldiers receive a formal briefing prior to selection so they know what they're getting into, but in my day we went in blind. It was for us to do our own intelligence gathering and try to prepare ourselves. The selection staff were, and are, the best of their generation, highly skilled at picking those with potential, not necessarily those that are the finished article.

The first four weeks test the soldier's physical and navigational abilities, and also personal qualities, such as fortitude and stoicism. There are what seem like endless marches in all weather conditions with differing weights on your back, from the heavy to the unbelievably heavy, and always including a weapon (also not light). If you survive the first three weeks, you move on to 'test week', when there are more marches – five timed ones on consecutive days with distances up to 28 km (17 miles). You have to pass at least four of those five marches before being allowed to undergo a final one, which is called, with no irony at all, 'Endurance'; a 64-km (40-mile) march carrying a 75-lb (5½-stone) Bergen (army rucksack), a weapon and any food or water you think you'll need on top of this. The completion time for Endurance varies, depending on weather conditions and the time of year, but if you are under the time by one second, you pass, and if you are over by one second, you fail.

A large proportion don't make the time, or suffer injury or voluntarily withdraw. Those that pass are sent on a three-week 'continuation training package', during which they're taught the basics of jungle warfare and how to operate in an SAS team.

Next is a five-week jungle phase. Now, the jungle can be all four seasons in one day, and each one extreme – wet, humid, boiling hot and freezing cold. You have to be aware of your own personal hygiene and health; insect bites and leeches take their toll, and a sick soldier is no use to anyone – in fact, he can be a burden to the rest of the team. The military tactics

required add to the mental and physical demands, as does being watched by instructors throughout.

As a student on the SAS course you also continue practising the basics; patrolling, close-quarter combat, observation posts, attacks and ambushes, with your skill set constantly being put under pressure by the instructors, who are assisting – and assessing – you. Then the assistance is taken away, and you're on your own. The training finishes with a testing exercise after which the students are selected (or not) by the staff. Injury will have continued to claim a number of victims, and still more will have de-selected themselves.

And those are just the first stages of selection.

I struggled throughout them. I'd been advised to wait a few years before attempting to take the course – I was six years younger than the average recruit – but I'd ignored that. Now, for the first time in my military career, I wasn't in the top 10 or even top 20 per cent of the fittest or most experienced. I had to fight to get to the front, working hard on both my fitness and navigation. I had to ignore my body's aches and pains (especially my back, knees and feet) and endure a number of setbacks where I only just made the times before I started to improve. Eventually I became one of only fourteen out of two hundred to pass the course.

Bouncing back from disappointment and dealing with pressure was vital. I coped because I told myself to take each day as a challenge, learn from my mistakes, and swear to do better next time. Having already been through a tough selection process with the Paras helped, but having my Super North Star was invaluable; knowing why we're suffering enables us to draw on reserves we didn't know we had, the power of purpose once again proving the key.

I was never going to take myself off this course – when doubts arose my internal voice loudly reminded me that this was something I'd wanted since I was thirteen years of age. One of the reasons for my success – such as it is – is that I may not be the most talented, but I will always be one of the most hardworking and disciplined. This, combined with my constant practising of basic skills, always helps.

'If you're going through hell, keep going.'
WINSTON CHURCHILL

Those who make it through the first stages of the course return to Britain – and yet another test: going 'on the run'. Participants have to evade a military unit, whose mission is to capture them, and then undergo hours of interrogation, during which they must stick to a specific script.

So, having made it through the initial stages of the course (I won't say with ease because that would be lying – let's say alive), I found myself in Second World War clothes – woollen jumper, cotton fatigues, no fancy fabrics here – freezing cold, soaked through and bitterly hungry, with a hundred-plus enemy force deployed to find us. There were fifty on the ground and the rest airborne in helicopters, both with all the modern equipment, such as night vision, that a contemporary force would allow.

This was now my last combat-survival assessment, a pass-or-fail moment. It was me and five other men, and our mission was to evade capture for a week. The weather was cold and wet and windy (in other words, Wales or Scotland)

and we'd each been given a rough, hand-drawn map with basic grid references and landmarks like forests, rivers and churches, so you could get your bearings, and, for guidance, a crude button compass you'd be disappointed to find in a Christmas cracker. And nothing else; no food, no shelter, no lighter, and if you were caught taking refuge in a nearby barn or farmhouse, you were failed instantly.

I knew one of the other men on this selection exercise, but the rest were army students. Using the map with the compass, I found us the best ground to move across until we slept, which meant on the ground, preferably in an indent, taking turns at sentry; one hour in four.

Every day we had to make checkpoints at a specific time and place. There, 'agents' would give us our next destination and information on the enemy who were tracking us. Sometimes they would offer us food: raw carrots or raw potatoes, once a raw pig trotter as a joke ('If you're hungry, chew on that!'). But no encouragement – your ability was being tested, they weren't on your side.

After updating our sketch maps, we were off again. The distance between landmarks was unknown, but the maps were enough to operate across difficult terrain. We were once very nearly caught, as my friend and I discovered that our group had, in our brief absence, responded to the bitter cold by lighting a fire; the smoke had been seen and a helicopter was circling. We hurtled back and explained to them very curtly that they had made a mistake and we would now have to dodge dogs and men all day long. Nevertheless, mistakes aside, we evaded capture for a week, until utterly exhausted, freezing cold and ravenously hungry, we made our final checkpoint as a team.

There were no celebrations – it wasn't that kind of triumph. Instead, we were loaded onto a truck and driven away; it was time for the interrogation phase – the final test – when we would employ the resistance to interrogation techniques we had been taught.

Name, rank, number and date of birth only – no matter what the interrogators said or did you just had to stick to that. I can't reveal any more, but let's just say it's difficult, testing and tiring; you have to keep reminding yourself why you want to pass and stay focused, determined and resilient. Most of us on selection passed this phase, though some did not, and, although this was not the end of the programme, the worst bits were now over.

Points for action: strengthening your warrior side

Do you exhibit the characteristics of a warrior? As before, score yourself out of 10, with 10 being perfect, and avoid using the number 7.

I can, and do, visualise what success looks like ☐

I practise my skills constantly ☐

I hold myself accountable for my actions ☐

I hold others in the team accountable for their actions ☐

I am able to focus on the here and now when I am in the pressure zone ☐

I seek improvement, not perfection ☐

I examine my mistakes to learn from them ☐

I am resilient and bounce back when I have a setback ☐

I know how to maintain my energy and passion to complete the task ☐

I can make decisions in the appropriate time frame and commit to those decisions ☐

I have good self-discipline ☐

I know when to lead and when to follow ☐

I am able to both lead and follow ☐

I am courageous and prepared to take a risk ☐

I totally commit to getting to each milestone I have set myself ☐

I can control my emotions when faced with a difficult situation ☐

I have a positive internal voice ☐

I trust my intuition ☐

I am able to train my mind like any other skill ☐

Are you reaching your full potential by keeping yourself physically fit and healthy?

The Warrior

My diet is healthy and varied ☐

My aerobic fitness is good ☐

My flexibility is good ☐

I ensure I am hydrated throughout the day ☐

My strength is good ☐

I monitor my fitness with technology ☐

I take time during my working week to recharge myself ☐

I spend quality time with my family ☐

I spend quality time with friends ☐

I spend quality time undertaking hobbies that are important to me ☐

I have relaxation techniques ☐

I get seven hours' sleep a night ☐

If you scored 0–4 in any area, that is a danger zone and must be improved, as it is a weak area for you and will undermine your performance. If you scored 5–7, there is room for improvement. If you scored 8–10, you're doing well!

Now calculate your overall average and the same rules apply.

What are your basics? Write down three to five skills you need to have in place so that even on your worst day you are difficult to beat. Think of ways to practise those things as often as possible, so that your performance in them is both the highest level it can be and instinctive.

Do you need to improve your physical fitness? Aim to incorporate a variety of exercises into your life:

☛ In theory, to be aerobically fit you only need to train three times a week for thirty minutes, including a warm-up and warm-down.

☛ Also, thirty minutes of strength training three times a week, working through different body parts, will help build your core muscle to ensure you minimise injury and assist your body to operate at a higher level of performance.

☛ Flexible muscles also help prevent injury; stretching your body in the morning, prior to exercise, and in the evening is one of the best ways to do this and should be done on a daily basis. Dance, yoga and Pilates are also ideal to improve flexibility.

☛ And it's not just about physical well-being: it's important to take time out as well. Try a simple twenty minutes of meditation. This will help you to declutter your mind of the many random thoughts it contains and focus on the most important ones.

Now start to consider the actions you will need to take in the next six months to start moving towards your first milestones on your life map. Think about what might stop you from taking action, including your own mindset, and how you will overcome that.

Once you start your journey, do you have the mental and emotional resilience to persevere through difficult times? When my resolve is being tested I have a mental routine that I go through to keep me on track. Everyone is unique, and you must devise one to suit your own needs, but to give you an example, here is my mental-resilience strategy:

☛ I always visualise what success will look like in any activity. I imagine being there in as much detail as I can.

☛ I plan for all the possible contingencies I can think of.

☛ I practice the appropriate skills I will need in the pressure zone.

☛ I take the time to rest and re-energise.

☛ I go to my key power words: courage/resilience/mindfulness/calm.

☛ I have power songs that motivate me ('Titanium' and 'Say My Name').

☛ I repeat my mantra in my mind: 'Don't ever jack'.

☛ I go through my focusing process, using my white, green, amber and red zones. (I will explain what these zones mean in the next chapter – see page 153.)

☛ I do not dwell on things that have happened in the past.

☛ I run through all of my previous successes in my mind to give me confidence.

☛ I embrace the unknown rather than being scared of it; not always having the answer keeps me sharp.

☛ I imagine what my mentors and heroes would do in the same circumstances.

☛ Finally, if I'm really about to step into the pressure zone and not confident I can get through it alone, I will ask for support from the people around me.

What similar things will help you stay focused on your goal? What power words will inspire you to keep going no matter what happens?

Embracing your warrior spirit is important on your road to success, but courage and action are much more effective with a good plan and a moral code to help you on your journey. So having identified your ethos, your strategy and your inner warrior, you now need to know how to balance all three so that you can achieve your Super North Star.

Chapter 6

Our Compass for Life in action

Approaching life by aligning the cardinal points of our Compass for Life can help us achieve our goals: knowing what we want (our Super North Star); knowing who we are, and what we are and are not willing to do to achieve what we want (our Ethos); preparing and planning how we are going to go about it (our Strategist); and taking action boldly and passionately (our Warrior).

As I have said, Alexander the Great was one of my earliest heroes. I remember a Ladybird book from when I was no more than eleven called *Alexander the Great: An Adventure from History*. It was vividly illustrated, with maps on the end-papers tracking all his campaigns. But it wasn't just about war, it was also about how he became a great warrior: how he was educated by Aristotle, how he cut the Gordian Knot, and how through military campaigns and conquests, he built an empire that stretched from Macedonia to India.

My favourite story as a boy was his taming of Bucephalus, a vicious and unmanageable horse. The horse was offered for sale to Alexander's father, King Philip, but he rejected it as wholly useless as no one could tame it – and then a lippy young Alexander spoke up. It was a shame to lose such an excellent horse, he said, just because no one was bold enough to handle him. The older men were, not unnaturally, put out. Alexander was challenged by his father. Could he do better? Alexander said if he couldn't ride the horse, *he'd* pay full price for it.

And he succeeded beautifully. Not by whipping or cursing Bucephalus, but by sneakily dazzling him with sunlight, mounting him in a single nimble leap, and then slowly drawing in the bridle, curbing his temper, until the horse was his.

'Without knowledge, skill cannot be focused. Without skill, strength cannot be brought to bear and without strength, knowledge may not be applied.'

ALEXANDER THE GREAT'S CHIEF PHYSICIAN

To a child, the idea that you could win round a horse and cock a snook at a king was absolutely inspiring. And there are many other stories and examples of his character. He didn't use brute force; it was all about respect (he often tended the wounds of his soldiers). As a strategist he had no equal, often defeating much larger armies or outmanoeuvring them; and as a warrior he led from the front and was himself wounded on numerous occasions. Even now I hold him up as the perfect example of combining a warrior and a strategist approach.

Balancing our compass

We need to develop the correct habits and attitudes in our ethos, our strategy and our warrior mode to propel us towards our purpose. When these are in harmony we will be at our best. Where people tend to struggle with this approach is by focusing too much on either strategy or warrior. But the warrior and the strategist are not separate; one may be stronger inside us than the other, but in that case we have to work harder to achieve balance.

Strategists use logic when they plan, looking at facts and risks. They seek solutions to problems, and remain open-minded until a decision is required. They hold themselves accountable. Warriors then put the plan into effect and lead the way towards each milestone. Once there, they reassess the situation, look to the next goal and move on in collaboration with the strategist.

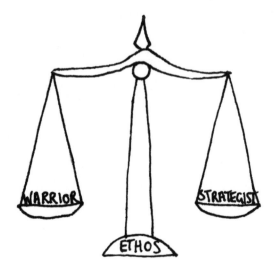

To succeed, we must be in control of both elements and switch seamlessly between the two, depending on the situation. And at our best we use our warrior and strategist aligned with our ethos, guiding our actions and decisions, as one single unit. We must know when to fight, when to plan, when to lead and when to follow. If we live in either area too much, we limit our development and harm our potential. Knowing this is a natural consequence of adopting the Compass for Life approach, and it is where our intuition comes into play. Once we know that we are giving equal weight to our strategist and warrior sides, in line with our ethos, we can begin to trust ourselves to make the correct decisions, knowing that we're no longer favouring action over planning, or vice versa.

'I have been impressed with the urgency of doing. Knowing is not enough; we must apply. Being willing is not enough; we must do.'

LEONARDO DA VINCI

On one occasion in the SAS, we had a wounded man, were 210 kilometres from safety, were surrounded by the enemy and needed a new strategy. So how did we respond?

We were flexible. As a team we were able to adapt to our difficult circumstances. We were innovative and did not conform to conventions. We established a defensive line, concentrated our force in the right direction, used the appropriate amount of aggression, and systematically gained control of the situation by attacking the weakest part of the enemy, turning it into a full-scale assault. This required a mixture of individual bravery and the group holding firm under fire.

We did not hesitate to support or challenge one another when things didn't seem right. Those who are called out must not take it personally. We knew when to be leaders and when to be followers. Roles change from one to another depending on the requirement: at times, I have called for assistance to defend a flank where I am in charge, and not much later have found myself having to support another group where I am reacting to another leader's directions.

The leader made a decision for us to break contact and move away from this location. We fully committed to that decision. Although it is important for everyone to have their say, once the leader has made a decision everyone must commit to it wholeheartedly. This is not about consensus or democracy, but about finding the best plan. We understood the need for efficiency: we had to leave some equipment behind, but we knew that the most essential equipment had already been packed away. We knew exactly what we needed to take and no more, which allowed us to be quick and nimble and cross terrain in the most effective way. By having a clear purpose alongside a combined strategist and warrior approach, we were able to emerge on top.

Seize opportunities

In life we are often torn between seeking our purpose and preserving our safety. Our need for safety is very powerful and can restrict us in our endeavours if we decline to take risks or seize opportunities that take us out of our comfort zone. If we are open to opportunities we will quickly find that we see them everywhere. Conversely, if we close our minds, we won't. If we adopt a combined warrior and strategist approach, it will help us to recognise opportunities that present themselves on our journey to our Super North Star, and have the courage to take action and grasp that opportunity.

'The desire for safety stands against every great and noble enterprise.'

PUBLIUS CORNELIUS TACITUS

I once spoke with a football manager who, in the early 1970s, at the age of seventeen, had the chance to join Arsenal and play in their first team. He turned it down because he didn't want to leave home and be away from his family. Arsenal went on to win the double (the league and FA Cup), while he returned to play for Huddersfield FC. He regrets this decision and wishes he'd been able to see what an incredible opportunity it was and had jumped at the chance.

It's important not to be glib about opportunities because, in many parts of the world, they're truly limited: women can't drive cars; men and women can't vote; people lack access to education, food and basic healthcare. Even in prosperous and more democratic countries, people's life chances are often circumscribed by conditions over which they have no control, and even those with the best of starts can grow up constricted by the expectations of others.

However, I think it's safe to say that unless you live in a dictatorship, failed state, deranged theocracy or war zone, there are plenty of opportunities surrounding you, probably more than you realise, and the biggest difference between individuals is whether they seize them or not.

The best soldiers I knew were all exceptional opportunity seizers; they were never flustered about which direction to take, or bothered if they only had a rough map. They knew their purpose and their end point, were happy to adapt and fill in the details of their journey along the way. They could either be a strategist or warrior depending on the needs of the situation.

In real life, few journeys have a clearly prescribed end point. All we can be certain of (apart from taxes) is that at some stage our lives will end. We just don't know when. So, to maximise our time, we need to keep healthy, enjoy life and remain alert to opportunities, as and when they present themselves – or, even better, go out and find them.

'It has long since come to my attention that people of accomplishment rarely sat back and let things happen to them. They went out and happened to things.'
LEONARDO DA VINCI

I was seventeen and in Alderney. My mum and dad had taken a risk and left Bradford for the chance to run a pub. This was my mum's dream, but Dad supported her, and left a job and friends he'd known all his life to do so. Having left school with only a handful of qualifications, I originally joined my parents with the intention of working in the pub and running the off-licence we'd also acquired. I had since moved out of home and was having the time of my life; it was summer, the island was full of tourists, I was renting an amazing house close to the beach, I was young, fit, and, best of all, I was on good money working seven hours a day. It was like living in a movie. A British one, admittedly, but about as much fun as a young man can have. And yet …

My Super North Star was twitching and I couldn't shake the feeling there was something else I should be doing. I was worried too, feeling a creeping concern that if I didn't act, I would miss out. I wasn't sure on what, but the pull was no less powerful for that. The feeling I should be doing something else grew stronger and stronger, until it presented itself fully formed: it was time for me to join the army.

Not yet eighteen, I was nervous about telling my parents, but they were not only supportive, they were pleased and proud of me. What I didn't know, and wouldn't find out till later, was that Mum was ill and they really needed me to stay. Six months later, they were forced to leave Alderney so she could be treated on the mainland, yet it never crossed their minds not to let me go.

Blissfully unaware, I crossed to the army careers office in Jersey, where I sat the initial tests in maths, English and general knowledge and passed with flying colours. Almost immediately I was offered a place on a course in Sutton

Coldfield and I was thrown – I'd imagined the selection process would take months and I'd see my summer out by the beach. But luckily I recognised it for the fantastic opportunity it was, and so, two weeks later, in a state of excitement, I was on my way to Sutton Coldfield, and, I hoped, to becoming a paratrooper.

When I and the other new recruits arrived, we were promptly told there was a new selection process; they'd made it even harder. Now if you wanted to join the Paras (as opposed to the infantry), it required a mile and half run in under 10 minutes, followed by a series of physical tests, such as seeing how many pull-ups (or 'heaves') and dips and sit-ups you could do. We were the first course to do this, and I passed, as did some others, but most failed as they'd not prepared for even this modest standard of fitness.

'Sail away from the safe harbour. Catch the trade winds in your sails. Explore. Dream. Discover.'

MARK TWAIN

I also found myself in the unusual situation where, having left school at sixteen with no one trying to stop me, I'd still done so well on the written tests that I was taken aside and offered a number of trades within the army: signals, mechanics, electronics, and the like. A succession of people tried to dissuade from joining the Paras, assuring me an apprenticeship was the way to secure my future. But although clearly all opportunities, they were not ones I wanted: they didn't point north for me. Two weeks later, I joined 472 Platoon in Aldershot and celebrated my eighteenth birthday in the Paras.

The greatest obstacle to success: fear

During our journeys, we will encounter many obstacles to overcome; life rarely runs smoothly and according to our plans. That is why we need to make sure we have chosen a Super North Star we are fully committed to; why we need to be well prepared, disciplined and courageous. So that no matter what happens in life, nothing can distract us or throw us off our course. We can remain focused on our target and keep moving forwards through any adversity.

One of the greatest obstacles on our journey is fear. It is the most negative emotion of all and is a constant companion on our journey. If stuck to our compass, like a magnet, it will quickly take us off course.

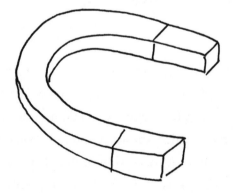

Fear can stop us from taking a chance, from leaving our comfort zone, from completing our mission. It can make us give up when we should persevere. It is the 'enemy' within, debilitating and confidence-destroying, and it can have significant consequences for our health if we allow it to. It can create havoc in our lives, inhibit everything we do or desire, and set us clearly on the path to failure.

Overcoming our fears once again comes down to approaching the situation as both a warrior and a strategist: looking at the situation calmly and logically, taking control of our minds and emotions, and finding the courage to act despite our fears.

'Nothing in life is to be feared, it is only to be understood. Now is the time to understand more, so that we may fear less.'

MARIE CURIE

So what is your greatest fear? I've asked that question hundreds of times and, whether to a ten-year-old child or the toughest soldier in the world and every sector in between, a common answer often emerges: FAILURE.

How we see ourselves and how we think others see us acts as a powerful influence on how we behave – peer group pressure is a clear example of this. We must understand that failure does exist, but we need to embrace it as an opportunity to learn, or the fear of it will hold us back. Failure is inevitable if we are to push ourselves to our limits.

I can't count the times I've had to dust myself down and pick myself back up. Or how many times people have tried to knock me off course to suit their needs, not mine. Our dreams should be big, and that always opens us to the possibility of failure. But that should not put us off.

Firstly, we must realise that failure should always be reframed as an opportunity to learn or a portal to success, a way to improve our performance. As long as we recognise this and make a quick mental assessment of what we could have done differently, we can close the gap on the goal we want to achieve in the future. But this means we have to be ruthlessly honest with ourselves and learn the lessons as quickly as possible.

Failure may be one key fear, but fear comes in many forms. So what is fear, and how can we overcome it? Fear is the thoughts we have when we feel a situation is a threat to our mental or physical well-being. Sometimes, such as in the case of an impending physical attack, it's entirely justified; other times, such as worrying what others think of us or obsessing over a perceived lack of skill, it is unproductive, bordering on self-harm. Unmanaged fear has the power to cripple our potential in all areas of our lives.

But fear also has a purpose, which is to protect us from danger, and our ability to sense danger is finely tuned. I once stepped on a snake in the jungle by accident and didn't even need to look down to know that it was a snake. My body reacted instantly and I sprang away from the danger while an annoyed snake slithered off into the undergrowth.

When our mind senses a threat, it floods our bodies with adrenaline, raises our heart rate, sharpens our senses and accesses reserves of energy so we can better fight or flee. But it can also make us freeze, rendering us unable to make decisions, leaving us helpless and hopeless in the face of a predator. The key is to take advantage of the former and not succumb to the latter. I once watched an entire group of soldiers listen to a lion roar at night in Kenya, shivering with apprehension that something big and powerful was prowling around, just as they were about to go out on a night patrol through its territory. But they certainly left the camp in a focused and very professional way that night.

To complicate matters, our responses aren't always based on reality. How often have we overreacted to an offhand comment or seen a snub in an email, or noticed young people in hoodies and thought we were in danger of being robbed, only for all of these reactions to be wrong? And did realising our mistake ever alleviate the fear the next time a similar situation arose?

I've experienced multiple kinds of fear: being worried about what my classmates thought of me; spending sleepless nights before giving a presentation; knowingly entering life-threatening situations; and, often worse, knowing I was about to send someone else into a life-threatening situation. It took me years to realise that controlling my reactions to the 'danger', whether real or not, and having a plan and being courageous, were all key to performing well.

'Fear makes the wolf bigger than he is.'
GERMAN PROVERB

One cold, wet day in Portland Harbour, Dorset, I had joined my SAS squadron's boat troop. We were practising the skills in which we'd need to be proficient, from canoeing to diving.

It was time for my diving proficiency test. I was taken to the side of the pier and my task was explained to me: I was to jump into the sea, then, when I hit the bottom, I would take my mask off. After a few seconds I would then place it back on and go through what is known as a 'clearing drill' – removing the seawater from the mask so I could see again. This meant pressing down on the top of the mask so that it lifted from my face, and then blowing through my nose so the air could force the water out.

Now, I had never dived before this moment, or even practised any aspect of diving, and I was nervous. Generally, beginners start off in a nice, warm, clear and totally safe swimming pool, so I was rather being thrown in at the deep end. The weight belt felt drown-worthily heavy as I laced it on. I put the mouthpiece in. I took a big gulp of air, mentally crossed my fingers and jumped. As soon as I hit the cold sea-water I started to sink to the bottom and panic flooded my mind. My thoughts went haywire: 'You're going to drown!' 'You're going to fail!' and, worst of all, 'What will people think?' My mind flashed back to my primary school swimming pool, but there was no Mr Edison to help me out this time, only water so freezing, cold and dirty I could barely see my hands in front of my face. I started taking in salt water through the breathing unit and my heart rate and breathing were racing like a terrified mouse.

The person supervising my test silently arrived next to me, as comfortable as a fish in water, and calmly assessed if I was panicking, while I promptly kicked up more sand and mud at the bottom, managing to further obscure my vision as I struggled to get a foothold.

I had to calm my thoughts.

With great effort, I refuted my panic with logic: I am not going to drown as I have access to air and can easily swim to the top. Yes, I am sinking, but not fast and, look, I have now stopped sinking. And, most importantly, nobody is concerned with me as they're too busy with their own thoughts and problems.

I began to calm down. Focusing on the task at hand meant I was left with just the thoughts I needed. I mentally talked the drill through to myself, looked at the instructor, counted to three, pulled off the mask, then placed it back on my head, full of salt water. I pressed down on the mask, blew through my nose and cleared the water. I had executed the 'clearing drill', got the thumbs-up and started my ascent. I was never so happy to break to the surface as at that moment. I passed that test and went on to complete a four-week dive course with the Special Boat Service. I now also had a great mental checklist to overcome my fears, which I have used many times since:

1. Examine the logic and the facts

2. Find the positives of the situation

3. Look at the risks without emotion

4. Accept the situation and act

'You have power over your mind – not outside events. Realise this, and you will find strength.'

MARCUS AURELIUS

Controlling our emotions

The real key to overcoming fear is to learn how to control our mind, emotions and thought processes. How much of what goes on in our phenomenal minds are we actually aware of? How much time do we spend training our minds to react the way we want when we need to perform well? If this is our command centre, surely we want to assess situations appropriately at a conscious and subconscious level so we can make the best decisions and win?

I first became aware of the voice inside my head when I started to push myself as a young sportsman. I can still remember the internal rows I had when fighting the desire to slow down or give up, which became most vocal when I started boxing; every time I stepped into the ring I seemed to bring with me an array of different fears, none of which were useful. And the voice in my head didn't restrict itself to matters of physical effort; there were times I was afraid of what people thought of me, and I worried about taking exams, public speaking and numerous other things.

Emotional control is critical. People are often surprised when I talk about emotions. I think maybe they convince themselves that soldiers don't have them, or, that if they do, it's a very narrow palette consisting of bravery, fortitude, suppression of fear and sadness, with maybe a few drinks thrown in at the end. To me emotional intelligence is critical; if we don't run our emotions, they will run us. If we don't understand our own feelings, motivations and biases, we will be forever out of control. But if we can understand how and why we behave the way we do, and what our strengths and weaknesses are, not only can we learn to control our own behaviour more effectively, we can also better understand others, and tolerate and even appreciate differences.

When I was younger, I had very little control over my mind and my emotions. I would spark up when there was the slightest provocation or my view of the world was challenged. I was close-minded to different perspectives, and too forceful with my own. It's why I'm grateful to have studied psychology; it opened my mind and enabled me to listen to other people's points of view and ways of doing things. It gave me the opportunity to see if their perspective was indeed better than mine. It allowed me to learn. I became aware that I didn't need to be afraid to admit I was wrong, which was an enormous release for me, and now I don't take it personally when I am challenged or someone disagrees with me. And, crucially, it allowed me to overcome my fears.

I only started to understand how to control my mind, rather than let it control me, when I went through Parachute Regiment selection, where we were told from day one: 'You don't jack, *ever!*' This mantra became so ingrained that, to this day, if I ever come close to stopping because something is too hard, or I'm too tired, or I don't think I'm good enough, the internal voice kicks in – 'You don't jack, *ever!*' – and I know to stay tough, keep going and never give up.

It was a cold, fresh summer's morning at Weston-on-the-Green in Oxfordshire. The mist was beginning to rise from the surface of the field. The stillness of the morning was broken by the creaking of the wire as a large silver barrage balloon was filled with gas and swelled into the air. The other young paratroopers and I watched it in complete silence. It was time for our very first parachute jump.

A none-too-sturdy-looking cage was connected to the balloon's underside by thin metal wires, designed to carry the four men who were due to jump out of it and an instructor who was there to make sure they did actually jump. The balloon was to lift the cage to a height of 800 feet (about the height of The Shard's viewing gallery, in London). Each jumper would be called in turn and told to stand at the entrance to the cage. The instructor would then call out a command sequence: 'Red on! Green on! GO!'

We watched the first group enter the cage, ready to be hoisted, when I noticed a friend was missing, one of the first people I'd met during training and one of the fittest and strongest students on the course. I asked an instructor where he was. 'Forget about him,' he said dismissively. 'He's jacked.'

No more explanation was given. This was not a good start to the day. I later found out that he'd decided the Paras wasn't for him and that he'd refused to jump. We lost one more that morning who also refused to jump. We were not allowed any contact with either of them and they were transferred to other infantry units. That kind of fear can spread quickly and cause others to doubt themselves.

My group was called and we stepped into the cage. I held on tightly as the balloon slowly lifted, and even in the cold morning I found I was sweating. Higher and higher, the balloon started to sway like we were at sea. The instructor looked like he was the only one clearly enjoying himself, pointing out local landmarks, such as the cemetery, in the distance. I was the last to jump and the voice in my head had had more than enough time to vividly picture all the ways I could die: the chute not opening and having to pull the reserve, both the chutes not opening ... and then my name was called.

I moved forward and stood in the doorway. Drills, contingencies and adrenaline raced through my mind, my heart pounded and, even with all my training, I had to try hard to make sure my legs did not shake.

In the heat of the moment, people do the bravest of things, but when we've had time to think, it takes a conscious effort not to balk. I'd wanted this too much and for too long to jack, so I ordered my mind to focus, went through my mental checklist, took in a deep breath and waited for the command: 'Red on! Green on! GO!'

And I jumped.

Following the drill we had been taught, I counted to three and looked up as my chute started to deploy. My stomach kept turning and I fell another 200 feet before it deployed fully and took enough air to stem the descent. Thank goodness, I said to myself, or something like that, and drifted to ground in one piece.

'Fear makes men forget, and skill that cannot fight is useless.'
BRASIDAS OF SPARTA

Finding our focus

Although it did get easier over the years, I would be apprehensive and need to focus before every jump, but I discovered a method that always helps me to overcome my nerves, creating four 'zones' that my mind goes through. It started off as a technique I used before having to jump, but I now use it before embarking on any dangerous or challenging activity.

The first is the 'white zone', where I do not need to focus on anything specific and my brain may be occupied by multiple thoughts. This is before I board the plane, where I am happy to chat about topics other than the upcoming jump. Second is the 'green zone', as I'm boarding the plane, where I start to focus on the generality of the task, activating the correct mental files relating to the performance. Third is the 'amber zone', where I am thinking about the specifics of the upcoming activity. As the plane approaches the drop zone, I begin to run through all the jumping drills in my mind. Last is the 'red zone', where I just do it. I forget about the outcome; that will take care of itself. I remind myself that I have honed my skills, that all I have to do is something I have done a thousand times in practice. I declutter my mind, and focus purely on my power words, such as 'stay tough' and 'courage'. No more thinking. I trust myself, and just do it.

Once I am in the red zone, fear never comes into it. Many people are surprised at that. But although, like any soldier, I have felt trepidation before a mission, once we were in the thick of it, fear has, for the most part, never entered my mind; I've always had too much to do. And I had other things as well, things that were much more important: my training and my team.

I doubt there are many people who have not struggled with doubt or fear at some moment in their lives. I feel sorry for anyone who has not, because they have a very difficult day coming their way at some time in the future.

'Courage is resistance to fear, mastery of fear – not absence of fear.'

MARK TWAIN

The thoughts in our minds are powerful: they can transform our view of the world for good or bad; inspire ideas that could transform ourselves and the world around us; or, conversely, distract us with fear or doubt and prevent us from achieving the things we want. We therefore need to ensure we have control over our thoughts, so that they don't become obstacles in our path.

Despite what Spock said in *Star Trek*, our logical mind is enhanced by our feelings, which are themselves a mixture of emotions and ideas. Understanding ourselves is key to controlling our feelings and is why a passion for what we are doing is vital to our success. When I see someone's passion, I know they're going to do well. Conversely, when I don't see the passion, I know they won't.

Passion, control, discipline, strategy, courage: all of these have always helped me to control any fears I might feel in an uncomfortable situation – and in the army, you encounter many of those.

'Courage is almost a contradiction in terms. It means a strong desire to live taking the form of readiness to die.'

G. K. CHESTERTON

It was 2300 hours on a cold November evening and I was working with a military unit. We were a few thousand metres over the Atlantic and we were about to jump into the sea to meet up with an O-class submarine (which have since been decommissioned).

There were eight of us wearing black diving suits with steerable parachutes on our back, reserve chutes on our front, life jackets around our neck, a pair of black fin-like flippers attached to our bodies and we each had a side knife (not to fight sharks with, hopefully, but to use if we got tangled up or needed it to cut ropes on the boat). We were lined up behind two black inflatable boats stacked on pallets with their own parachutes and all of our equipment on board, ready to move on the rollers they were resting on. After they'd been pushed out of the C130 Hercules, we'd follow, aiming to land as close to the boats as possible, and then RV with the submarine. We broke the cyalume sticks on the side of the boats to make them easier to see, and did the same with the ones on our arms. We'd practised this drill many times.

The inside of the aircraft glowed red to minimise the light pollution and help our eyes adjust to the darkness as it dropped to a thousand feet. The parachute jump instructor called us forward. A silence fell as each man checked his parachute line and ensured it was hooked to the metal wire on top of the fuselage that ran the entire length of the plane. It was this configuration that would drag our chutes out as we jumped. Each man was lost in his own thoughts, going through his own drills. My mind started to focus on the task at hand. For a moment I felt the apprehension I always had before I jumped. It's not fear, I told myself, I always feel this way before engaging in any dangerous actions. I instructed myself to think clearly; I was going to jump, so there was nothing to worry about. How could I refuse? I'd never live it down. Plus, I was the group's leader, so I needed to look at least a little bit confident.

The back door of the Hercules opened and cold air and noise rushed in. The wind speed was 12 knots, just within safe limits for parachuting at night. My heart started to beat faster; that element of danger again. It was pitch black and the sea would be rough. There was no safety boat in attendance.

Luckily, although jumping out of a plane was potentially dangerous, I had parachuted with boats many times, so I knew what to expect. I went through my checks and thought not about the danger itself, but about what I needed to do at the next stage, which was to land in the sea and get to the boat as fast as I could. I visualised what I needed to do: I could see myself cut away my parachute before I hit the water; swim to the semi-inflated boats; cut away their parachutes and the pallet they were attached to; inflate the boats fully; and finally prepare for meeting the submarine. As I was waiting for the signal to start the sequence of actions, my mind began to focus. I decluttered my mind using key words such as 'stay tough' and 'courage'. I reminded myself I had done this many times before and that this gave me confidence.

Then the jump instructor told me the wind was gusting over 12 knots, which meant the jump could be cancelled.

A few of the team glanced at me hopefully – fear can make us look for the easiest option rather than the correct one – but they knew instantly from the look on my face that we were going to jump. Of course, what they didn't know is that the same thought was going through my mind: I could stay in the aircraft and *not* jump. So why did I keep putting myself through something this scary? I readily countered these questions with my prepared responses: 'Because I love doing this' and 'It's what keeps me alive'.

I told the jump instructor that we'd still jump unless he called it off.

I looked around the team and saw the focus etched into their faces. I paid particular attention to one of our team, who I knew hated parachuting. CT was terrified of it and had to force himself to jump out of the aircraft. Knowing the jump was taking place in weather conditions that were the limit for an operation was not helping him.

A great way to alleviate our fears is discussing them as a group. This can be difficult if we worry what others may think about us if we confess our vulnerabilities, but admitting to them frees us of many constraints. I certainly found that learning to say I was scared of a situation was liberating because only then could I acknowledge the difficulties and come up with solutions.

As I looked at the team, I saw men who were bonded by shared experiences, having survived dangerous situations together. We didn't all like each other but we respected one another and we knew we were all in this together.

I love it when a team take strength from one another and are willing to put aside personal achievement for the greater good. They have a team ethos and no one wants to let their teammates down. They have a common motto around which they align. The SAS has 'Who Dares Wins.' The Paras have 'Utrinque Paratus' (Ready for Anything).

I looked back at CT, who was looking scared, and he gave me a nervous smile. I moved across to him and asked him if he had made a will yet. Laughter is often the best medicine in these situations.

The jump instructor loudly called out the two-minute warning and the plane descended further, lining up to the drop zone. As it was two minutes before we had to jump out of the plane, the atmosphere inside changed and everyone was now fully focused on what they had to do. My attention moved to the two lights in the plane; the red one to warn us and then, a moment later, the green light to signify we were about to jump.

The instructor yelled 'Red on!' and the red light came on. Moments later he yelled 'Green on!' The boats were pushed forward and fell into the blackness and, one by one, we followed into the dark. My chute opened, which is always a nice feeling, and I looked around for the boats below us. Seeing the lights below, I directed my chute to land as close as I could. The wind was strong so I turned my chute into it to slow me down. Before I hit the surface, I opened a side of my chute so that it fell and collapsed. I dropped into the water and went under; the water was cold and the waves high and I came to the surface and got out of the chute as quickly as I could and swam across to the boat. One of the team arrived at the same time and we cut away the boat's parachute and packaging, which slowly sank into the sea. We inflated the boat and put on the engines as the other two in our team arrived. The water was too rough to meet the sub; we would have to wait until it calmed down.

We now had the teams in both of the inflatable boats and calmly waited for the sea conditions to subside. We brought the boats alongside one another and tied them together to give us greater stability. Fortunately, an hour later, conditions abated enough for us to go through the next drill – otherwise it would have been a long night waiting at the rendezvous point. The submarine had been in the area for a while and, with its sophisticated monitoring devices, it had been able to track us easily. It now came past us with its periscope up, so we could see it and then follow in its wake. It was dark, but we had some moonlight to assist us. Then the conning tower burst out of the sea, just enough so we could come behind it and continue to follow. We used a special device to connect our boats to the conning tower so that, as it rose further out of the sea, we could land our boats on its back. However, one mistake and we'd fall off the side. That was when my heart started to race again and everyone's attention was back on the task at hand.

Pete, who was in charge of this procedure, was new to the team and had only done it before in practice. He sat at the front of the inflatable, poised to connect us to the tower. The other boat was connected to the rear of ours and we moved in unison like a slalom team carving our way through the waves until we were close enough for Pete to connect us up. The waves kept buffeting us back and forth and, just as he was about to connect … he dropped the device into the sea. He looked at me forlornly, but we had prepared for this contingency, so I simply gave him the spare set and told him, 'Right, that's the practice over with.'

He smiled and completed the procedure and we landed on deck. Two minutes later, as we rested on top of what I think is one of the most beautiful boats in the world, the sun started to rise and the hatch opened, with one of the officers in charge and his men ready to assist with the next stage. The two boat teams didn't even notice the sunrise as they set to stripping the boats down in a precise manner and, within five minutes, the boats were packed away into the submarine.

We then went below decks. There is always euphoria when you overcome doubts or fears. The teams were pleased with themselves as we had just successfully completed a very complicated and dangerous task. Each man had had to deal with the voices inside his head and had found ways to perform to the best of his ability and, most importantly, we'd had the team's mental toughness to guide us as well.

I can't count the times someone has just patted me on the back to let me know I am doing the correct thing, or given me the thumbs-up when I needed support. It has helped me to deal with my inner doubting voice and look at all situations as an opportunity to learn something new. I now know that there is nothing wrong with being scared when faced with a difficult situation or simply the unknown. As long as I have prepared, planned and practised, I know I can throw myself into the task 100 per cent, stay focused, and trust my internal voice and my intuition to see me safely through to the other side.

When we understand and can overcome our fears, we can really start to make progress towards our Super North Star. And as we move ever closer, we should always make sure that we continue to keep our compass balanced between our cardinal points.

Points for action: balancing your compass points

Are you balancing your warrior, strategist and ethos? As before, score yourself out of 10, with 10 being perfect, and avoid using the number 7.

My ethos is always at the heart of any decision I make, both as a strategist and warrior ☐

I see myself as a strategist ☐

I see myself as a warrior ☐

I am able to remain both detached in creating my strategy and passionate in getting to each milestone as a warrior ☐

I can visualise both long- and short-term objectives ☐

Even in warrior mode I am always aware of the strategy and its overriding objectives ☐

Once I have formulated a strategy, I take immediate action ☐

If the facts of a situation change, I do not hold on to outdated ideas in either mode ☐

Our Compass for Life in action

I know when to lead and when to follow in either mode ☐

I can communicate effectively in either mode ☐

I am energised and positive in either mode ☐

I am creative and can think outside of the box in either mode ☐

If you scored 0-4 in any area, that is a danger zone and must be improved, as it is a weak area for you and will undermine your performance. If you scored 5-7, there is room for improvement. If you scored 8-10, you're doing well!

Now calculate your overall average and the same rules apply.

Based on the questions above, if you think that you favour one aspect of your compass over the other, think about what you can do to balance them.

If you are confident that you have your compass well balanced, think about what scares you in life. Write your fears down – they can be general fears or specific to your purpose. How can you overcome those fears? Think also about any opportunities you feel you have missed so far in your journey through life. Do you still regret them? What can you learn from your experiences to make sure you are open to opportunities in the future?

———————————————

With all this in mind, and your life map now teeming with ideas and inspiration, you should be ready to embark on your journey towards achieving your purpose. Before you get started, there is one more important element that can help you succeed: teamwork.

Chapter 7

Working as a team

Successful people who operate alone are a very rare commodity indeed. Any person who wishes to fulfil their purpose will need a team around them, a support network, whether that's friends, family or colleagues. In other words, people who can help us overcome difficulties and stay focused on our path. How we select and interact with that team or support network is key.

Our personal support network

When I first decided to leave the SAS and make my first foray into business, I made a mistake I now teach others not to, which was failing to tell the people closest to me what my purpose was so they could support me.

It was different when I was a young man. Self-absorbed and self-contained, I could change my mind on a whim and it would affect nobody but me; I could go to the beach, stay out late, train hard or take it easy, and the only person I had to discuss it with was me. They were the easiest negotiations of my life. It's one thing when a situation affects only ourselves (and that's certainly rare in a negotiation), but it's quite another when it affects our family, children, team or organisation. We then need to consider the others around us, ask for their opinions and listen to their advice.

I recently worked with a group of ten-year-old children who went home with their Compass for Life and asked their parents some challenging questions about their own journey and their family compass. The decisions we make can affect us a family unit, so it is important that everyone understands the purpose, has the same values, is working with the same strategy and the same passion.

Frankly, in my case, I needed help to pursue my goals and for me that meant my family. But first I had to actually include them in my plans – people are not as psychic as we'd like. I had to explain to them what I wanted, which was quite humbling, especially as, when I told them, we all realised that I had not included them in my thoughts, and they were quite shocked (I had some explaining to do that night, I can tell you). To be successful, we have to take our support network with us; it is rare to get to the top without the help and support of the people around us.

Our team compass

The Compass for Life is also not just intended for individuals. These principles apply to teams as well, whether in business, the army, sport or any endeavour that requires a team of people working towards a common goal. For a team to be successful, it still needs to have a purpose, an ethos, a strategy and a warrior attitude to taking action.

In the SAS, on every mission, those were the principles we adopted. Our starting point would have been months of training beforehand. We trained with various weapon systems from anti-aircraft equipment to mortars and ensured that we had the most up-to-date intelligence on the enemy and practised our basic skills constantly.

We understood the enemy's ambitions and their Achilles' heel; where they were weak and where they would fracture under pressure. We knew more about their typical behaviour in combat than they did, having studied their cultural norms, their motivations, their psychology, integrity and emotional intelligence, their training and physical resilience and their leadership. They often hadn't done the same with us.

We trained in similar environments to the ones we would operate in so we were familiar with the ground and conditions and were confident in our abilities to defeat the enemy wherever and whenever we met. This was not arrogance or an underestimation of their capabilities; it was an honest review. We would, however, treat them as if they were our strongest enemy so we would not lose the edge in battle and be underprepared.

Prior to any deployment, each person refreshed his individual skills (explosives, medical capabilities, signals, languages and numerous others) and some studied the advanced skills that might help with this particular deployment, such as heavy weapons training. We refreshed our standard operating procedures. We practised repeatedly for every contingency we could think of until it became second nature.

Everyone knew their own role and also knew each other's key roles, so if someone was injured, another person would simply step in and cover their position. Communication is vital under pressure: when time is of the essence, why use ten words when we could use one? We'd got to the point where we could communicate with each other by the briefest of nods or simply use hand signals. We'd prepared in the pressure zone, with another team playing the part of the enemy, and using live ammunition and explosives, distraction devices, smoke and fire to create difficult environmental conditions.

We were a team; and we operated like a well-oiled machine, able to deal with whatever obstacles came our way because we had a clear common purpose (defeat the enemy); an agreed team ethos (trust and support one another); a clear strategy (we knew our enemy and had prepared for all contingencies); and we were warriors (skilled, disciplined and ready to step boldly into action).

The best warriors have enormous energy and passion for what they do and want to work with like-minded spirits, who they can trust and respect. The resulting *esprit de corps* creates a team dynamic and a special strength. As Chief Tecumseh, leader of the Shawnee, put it: 'A single twig breaks, but the bundle of twigs is strong.'

Selecting our team

The first obstacle to overcome is the selection of a team – finding the right people and figuring out how to make them work together is a skill in itself.

It takes discipline and time to hire the right people; we have to ensure the selection process is fair, and that it allows candidates to show the qualities and skills we require to the best of their abilities. We then have to put those skills under pressure to see if they are deep-rooted and sustainable.

The SAS's selection process has not changed for generations, with good reason; it's as objective and as measurable as possible. Where it is subjective, say on attitude or behaviour, decisions are made as a group to minimise the possibility of bias. Over the years, people have argued that not enough candidates get through, and have suggested lowering certain criteria. But most of those who fail simply give up because they lack the self-discipline to stay the course.

The goal is to select the right people. The skill set is important, but always second to attitude. When in doubt, do not hire, wait. I was recently asked to sit on an interview panel. We watched six candidates go through a tough role play, present their vision for the future of the organisation, complete a written module, and prepare a road map for the organisation to cover the next three months.

One candidate stood out to me, the youngest by far. Although he had a few rough edges, he also had an enormous amount of energy, intellect and emotional intelligence. He scored the highest in the group and, when asked, others on the panel agreed he was talented, approachable, with a tough side as well as a sense of humour (essential). But another candidate was already a favourite, and was already in the position as a temporary measure. He had done well, but was average.

When the panel discussed the day, I immediately noticed that they became subjective, bringing in age and other variables as issues, and it was even suggested that the young candidate might ruffle a few feathers within the organisation. I pointed out they were in danger of choosing a safe pair of hands over a star of the future. What did that say about the company? With a little more objectivity, the young candidate got his opportunity, but it took a disciplined approach to get the correct result.

'Hire character. Train skill.'
PETER SCHUTZ

We must also beware of selecting people because they are like ourselves; it's easily done. I once knew a very talented coach who could not stop picking one particular player. I took him to one side and asked him why, given that the player failed time and again. We danced around the subject until he admitted the player reminded him of his younger self.

Equally, just as we must be aware of overlooking mistakes because we like someone, we must also be vigilant about constantly finding fault with someone we dislike. When I was once in charge of a military selection process, I noticed an instructor took a clear dislike to one of the candidates. I watched with interest as he pointed out every mistake. And so, every time the candidate did something well I pointed it out too. Not only to the instructor in question but to other instructors too.

At the first assessment, I was not surprised to hear all of the instructors tell me how badly the candidate had done. I acknowledged their concerns: 'Let's agree everything you have said is true.' And then I changed tack. 'But explain why you've not mentioned anything good about this soldier? He's managed to stay the course and not given up, and I've noted numerous occasions when he's performed well, and have pointed those times out to you and not one of you has brought it up.' I paused for effect (we were in a jungle camp, it was dark with only the light from torches and the noise of wildlife in the background, so the effect was pretty impressive). The instructors fell silent. I simply said, 'I want this soldier to be judged on his performance and attitude and nothing else. I expect him to be judged fairly.' I didn't say anything else. I didn't need to. The student passed and went on to do extremely well.

What we look for in a person will vary according to what specific skill set we need, of course, but there are some general character traits that will always be an asset:

- General competence
- Self-awareness, emotional intelligence and communication skills
- Physical resilience
- Courage
- Integrity
- Humour
- The ability to lead or to follow as necessary
- Motivation and energy
- A desire to achieve and learn
- Mental toughness

With the right people we can create a high-performance environment. With the wrong people we won't.

'First-rate people hire first-rate people; second-rate people hire third-rate people.'

LEO ROSTEN

Once we have the right people, we also have to let them get on with it. Only a fool hires people to do a job and then micromanages their every move. In all of the operations I have been involved in, once we were given a purpose, we were left to do it without interference, only support. I am fortunate because I have come across people who empower others in the military, sports and business. They allow their people to do their job and only keep an overview. If we have selected and developed the best people, why would we not empower them? Sadly, I have also come across a lot of organisations that do not understand that concept at all.

Of course, we can't always pick our team at the outset. Sometimes we have to take the cards as they fall. On numerous occasions I've moved to different sectors within the army to head a new team. In these cases, the group and I had to accelerate our ability to cooperate because, in most cases, we were operational, which meant we could be called upon at a moment's notice to deploy anywhere in the world on active service.

And since leaving the SAS to work in the business world, I've had to create teams with people who have only been through a rudimentary interview process. That then requires setting aside time to get to know each individual and for them to get to know one another. I ask people about their personal journey to date so that I may understand their background, family, motivation, mentors, super-strengths and areas they may want to enhance.

Bringing team members together

When I haven't had control over the team selection, I first look to establish common denominators: our purpose, our ethos, our strategy and our warrior spirit. I then look to try to develop people within the team to the highest standards possible. It still comes down to getting to know people, understanding their particular strengths and weaknesses, finding the best place for them to operate, and figuring out how we can make everyone come together to work as an unstoppable team.

I then look to develop the influential people in the team; I call this 'force multiplying', because I can achieve more through the influential people who support the team's ethos, strategy and purpose. I then look to bring the disruptive people (if there are any) on board with the team outlook, or look for positions best suited to their talents and attitude elsewhere if they are not compatible with the team. I try to do this with the utmost compassion, but I will remove them in a heartbeat if necessary.

In order for a team to be able to adopt the Compass for Life approach, they have to be willing to work together, to find a shared purpose and ethos that they can all agree and commit to, and to work together as warriors to achieve success.

To achieve that, we need to create a sense of comradeship. We don't necessarily have to like each other, but we do have to respect and, crucially, trust one another. The best way to do that is to understand each other, to find common ground. I need to be in a team with people who care for me and understand what makes me tick. I want to be in an environment where people are concerned for my well-being and push my potential.

In my twenties, if you'd asked me if I understood my team, I would have instantly said, 'Yes, I know them well.' Sadly, in reality, I would only have known them at a superficial level. I may have known their skill set, but I never took the time to fully understand what made them tick, or how to use their super-strengths more effectively, or how to minimise any weaknesses they had.

Next, we need a shared purpose. This is essential. Why would I follow a purpose I do not believe in? If I am included in it I feel significant, especially if I have influenced the plan in some way.

Once all of these elements are in place, I try to build deeper levels of trust by encouraging debate and challenges within the group, and by making sure the team supports one another and holds one another accountable for the delivery of the standards and performance they have agreed to. This accountability is key, as it allows the team to move to another level of performance.

I recently went back to work with a group of international sportsmen whom I had worked with for a number of years. I had not been with the group for over ten months and, when I watched them over a period of three days, I noticed that they had lost that critical edge teams need to perform at the highest standards – they had become complacent. As we went through the programme, I pointed out where in the past the players and coaches would not have accepted certain behaviours or any drop in standards, in either performance or attitude.

The leadership team and the players quickly realised that they had been taking easier options in training, not deliberately, but because they were only slight infringements they thought such a small slip didn't matter and, as a result, standards had started to drop inch by inch. Within a few days of realigning, their attitude and standards moved back to the appropriate level and they returned to being a high-performing team.

'Remember, upon the conduct of each depends the fate of all.'
ALEXANDER THE GREAT

Team members should never let their comrades down. The most dangerous weakness for a team that I have observed is when a warrior doesn't follow the game plan. Instead of exercising discipline and control, they overreact, fail to do the basics well, are selfish and don't communicate with others. Lacking humility, they're only concerned with their own survival, and are the most likely to quit and then lay blame at anyone's door but their own. Such weakness can infect an entire group and create internal chaos. I have seen this in every walk of life. I love the All Blacks' mantra, as James Kerr notes in his book *Legacy*: 'No matter how good a player is, we do not have dickheads on the team.' Words to live by.

For a team to work well together, every individual needs to feel as though they are being heard. Any member can come up with new and different ideas, which is why the SAS lets every member have a voice. And so must we. Because, I can assure you, there will be some people in our teams who are geniuses.

The SAS has a classless structure, but it is not 'rankless'. There is still authority. Which means everyone has a voice, but it is not a democracy; leaders may listen but they will ultimately have to take the final decision themselves (although in all my time as a leader I have only had to go against my team on two occasions; generally my team gave me a better plan or enhanced the one I had).

We also removed key individuals at certain times during SAS training so that individuals and teams got used to being leaders and making decisions. We had a testing scenario where mistakes were not tolerated and there were team consequences for making them. This type of training encourages mental toughness in individuals and teams. By the time we were finished, all of us could lead or follow if necessary. We trusted one another. We knew our strengths and had identified those weaknesses that could be a distraction.

Leadership

Where the team really differs to the individual in the Compass for Life approach is the need for leadership to direct the team's efforts, and to ensure that no one is straying from the agreed course. Leadership is a key part of success. In most teams, we will need to learn both how to lead and how to follow. When it is our turn to lead, there are certain traits which we need to have to be effective, which make people want to follow us, and which bring out their best performances.

'The task of leadership is not to put greatness into humanity, but to elicit it, for the greatness is already there.'

JOHN BUCHAN

Communication

Leaders know how to adapt their style and tone where necessary. If we can't get our message across, then having a message doesn't even matter. One of the best communicators I know is negotiator Dr Rob Kennett, who has saved countless lives. From him I learned how to lead without authority, how to make a good first impression, how to connect emotionally with people and build trust so that you can influence their behaviour. It's the opposite of bullying. We need to take every opportunity to understand the needs of our team, and forgive honest mistakes. And once mistakes are dealt with, we mustn't keep bringing them up. Nothing undermines people's confidence like being reminded they've failed before.

Knowledge

The best leaders know how much they don't know. They learn from their mistakes and learn from others. They never isolate themselves from their teams or hide from bad news. I am fortunate to be working with three CEOs in their late fifties who still take on new challenges and continue to learn new skills so as to keep themselves at the top of their professions.

Discipline

Leaders need the discipline to lead by example; it is important to exhibit the same behaviours and standards that we expect from our team. 'Don't do as I do, do as I say' didn't work on us when we were children; it won't work with adults either.

'Setting an example is not the main means of influencing others; it is the only means.'
ALBERT EINSTEIN

Courage

We need to stay strong in adversity and develop our risk tolerance. But be aware, this is when leadership can become difficult and lonely, and when we can doubt ourselves.

One of my best friends had to make a call as to whether to ground a number of planes due to a suspected terrorist threat. The decision was monumental – especially if he was wrong! Closing planes down and disrupting flight paths would cost a lot of money and involve a number of foreign countries. The problem was there were no solid facts to support his decision. It came down to him trusting his instincts and experience. He acted courageously, made the call and saved a lot of lives. With courage, everything is possible; without it, nothing is.

Listening

Leaders always try to develop themselves and others. They surround themselves with people who both challenge and support them on many different levels. Bad leaders surround themselves with a court.

Remaining calm

Always look for solutions, not excuses, and know that losing our temper has never found a lost key, caused someone to return a call, or stopped a car from breaking down. Sometimes things go wrong. How we deal with it is a test of our character. We can all be calm and pleasant when times are calm and pleasant.

Commitment

Leaders ensure everything they do is focused towards their goal.

'Leadership is a matter of intelligence, trustworthiness, humaneness, courage and discipline ... When one has all five virtues together, each appropriate to its function, then one can be a leader.'

SUN TZU

Leadership is a fragile skill, and one on which the success of the team hangs. I've been lucky enough to be encouraged and inspired by leaders my whole life.

I had just joined the Paras when Major Dick Trigger arrived to take over as our company commander. He was as fit as us (if not fitter), highly intelligent and, like Alexander the Great, did everything he asked of us. His purpose was clear: to make us the best company within the battalion and develop us as people and as soldiers.

We were on a major exercise in Scandinavia, run by the colonel of the regiment, and had been tasked with clearing a valley defended by the enemy (in reality, B Company).

There was, as always, great rivalry between each company and we were the last to go through. Having watched half a dozen groups precede us, B Company thought they knew what to expect as we moved off, traversing the valley to the start line.

They were wrong. Trigger had watched the other groups too and, at the last minute, called some of us aside with new orders; one platoon was to break off and attack from an unexpected direction. He explained he would distract the enemy by firing on different positions and by moving troops around to attack outposts so that the enemy would be unsure which direction our attack would be coming from. We checked our maps; his chosen route was difficult and would take at least four to five hours of loaded marching and climbing to get around the terrain. Trigger said he'd wait to attack until we were in position. We set off as a snowstorm started, and the colonel, unable to see us, became increasingly frustrated; this was not going to plan and time was running out. Via his staff, he ordered Trigger to move us off, but Trigger refused. So the colonel turned up and made his demands in person. Trigger refused and explained: 'I wouldn't do this for real and I do not intend to do it now.' As it was a training exercise, the colonel did not issue an explicit order that he was bound to follow, and Trigger had the courage to stick to his convictions, as any good leader must. He waited and waited and resisted pressure, until we were exactly where he wanted us. Only then, with the enemy facing the wrong way, did he attack.

We easily overpowered B Company and won with minimum casualties. A great lesson in behaving in practice as you would do for real.

Trigger created a passion to succeed, and succeed we did, time and time again – later winning a 'march and shoot' competition against all the other countries on the exercise. And he was a humble man who always passed the credit on to us. Most inspiring to me, and the reason I was able to become the man I am, was his determination to fight for us.

'If your actions inspire others to dream more, learn more, do more and become more, you are a leader.'

JOHN QUINCY ADAMS

We are surrounded by good leadership all the time – a well-run restaurant, a business that delivers what and when it says it will, doctors and nurses in A&E making life-saving decisions daily – but most of the time we don't notice it. That's a shame, but it's much more dangerous if we don't recognise bad leadership.

Beware the 'charismatic' leader

He was six foot two, powerfully built and a wonderful orator. He was a master of all media; radio, television, newspapers, social media. He captivated his nation with his words – moving, lyrical and almost poetic as he spoke of his people's glorious courage and a culture that stretched back genera- tions. When he told his audience that greatness beat in their hearts, they believed him. When he told them they were disciplined, truth-telling and independent-minded, they believed that too. He told them they were special almost as often as he told them they'd been wronged. How their pov- erty was not their fault, nor an accident of fate.

He told them he was one of them; a warrior who'd fought in battles and was, as he stated numerous times, 'prepared to die for my country'. He promised them hope and tri- umph and justice. Everything they'd lost would be returned to them and more. And they each had a part to play in this story – together they'd build a future their children and grandchildren would be proud of.

He was as eloquent and as charismatic a leader as I have ever come across.

One of my greatest pleasures was seeing him arrested as a war criminal.

I can't tell you what he did.

I can't tell you where he's from

I can't tell you what *I* did.

But I can tell you this: I've met him a dozen times in a dozen countries and he's always the same: vain, shallow, violent and vindictive. And he always gets found out. And he always gets caught. But not before damage has been done.

The words used to describe bad leaders are the same whatever their role. They do not listen; it's all about them; their policies are based on 'one style fits all'; their attitude is constantly one of 'you're either for us or against us'; they lack accountability and use scapegoats; they're paranoid, inconsistent and cynical; they divide and rule, creating a culture of fear; they're susceptible to flattery and surround themselves with lackeys; they take credit for other people's ideas; they overreact to any challenges to their authority, and punish according to their mood, not the facts.

That's not to say, however, that they have no talents. That's what makes them so dangerous. They are frequently charming and charismatic; they can get people to say and do things completely out of character; they operate well under pressure; and they have a very clear purpose, which they pursue with courage, focus and discipline.

If bad leaders simply wore a black hat and a badge that

said 'evil' it would, of course, make all our lives easier. But they don't.

'You do not lead by hitting people over the head – that's assault, not leadership.'

DWIGHT D. EISENHOWER

Of course, you don't have to be evil to be a bad leader. One of the worst leaders I have come across managed to crush an entire platoon's *esprit de corps* within ten minutes of taking charge.

He arrived one morning having been away for two years on secondment to another infantry unit in the north-east, ironically to practise his leadership skills. He strode confidently into our barracks and, without asking our names, or introducing himself save his name, rank and experience, announced that we weren't working hard enough, that a new regime was called for – and he intimated that some of us would be leaving if we did not step up to the mark.

He didn't ask us how we felt. He didn't give us a sense of purpose – a 'why' – he just told us we were sub-par and there would be consequences for those who did not toe the line. Those in our group who had known him before were as shocked as those of us who'd never met him. It was collectively disturbing because we were sure we were good. We had been consistently successful, had a powerful sense of camaraderie, had done all that was asked of us and would have died for each other without question.

But his agenda of control by fear left some very tough soldiers feeling isolated and vulnerable. No one wanted to be the one who let the side down, the one who got kicked out. Collectively our body language changed, our trust became strained and we became cautious and overly careful when communicating as a team. We were no longer a unit. We became a collection of men who began to do just enough. Some looked to leave and some of us even became disruptive, doing the opposite of what we were asked.

Then, after watching him throwing his weight around once too often I realised it wasn't a display of strength but of a lack of confidence. Like every bully he was frightened his inadequacies would be found out and was covering his own shortcomings by inventing ours. A number of us rebelled against his leadership when he tried to isolate us.

'The standard you walk past is the standard you accept. That goes for all of us, but especially those who, by their rank, have a leadership role.'

LIEUTENANT GENERAL DAVID MORRISON

Mental bullying is a clear ethos failure and is, in many ways, worse than physical bullying because the victim can replay situations and recreate bad feelings time and time again. Fortunately, once I realised what his game was, I started to feel sorry for him and would laugh internally and, unfortunately on one occasion, out loud, at his most outrageously counterproductive behaviour. While this didn't always help, it meant from a strategic perspective that it stopped my warrior spirit stepping in and doing something I might have regretted.

The path to success

With good leadership and a cohesive team, working together as a unit – with a purpose, an agreed ethos, a well-planned strategy and a combined warrior spirit – we can achieve the highest standards and performance, and, even on our worst day, we will be difficult to beat.

A few years ago I was part of a group – fifteen in all – operating behind enemy lines. Our foray was the first in a number of offensive and intelligence-gathering operations and it had taken us weeks to get there. The first part of the journey had been by plane, the next by helicopter, then, after hiding for two weeks, we sneaked in, and we kept on sneaking until we were some 200 km (124 miles) behind enemy lines. We were operating under every soldier's preferred directive – a chaos directive. In layperson's terms it meant that once we had identified our targets, we had free rein to blow up and destroy as many of them as possible – convoys, military facilities, telephone lines, fuel dumps – with the added proviso that we were to 'gain intelligence to assist the main war effort elsewhere and capture any high-ranking soldiers'. And we had freedom to achieve this in any way we saw fit without having to ask for permission. A simple and clear Super North Star that gleamed like a lighthouse through the fog of war.

Our night goggles cast the desert a sickly green as we

worked through the night, quietly observing enemy positions and tracking their movements. Our strategy and our purpose were clear, and each man knew exactly what he was expected to do and achieve.

But, in our heightened state of excitement, we stayed slightly too long in one of the zones we were responsible for, and first light came quickly upon the horizon. And one of the downsides of free rein is that there is no calling for help; we were on our own.

With time running out and unable to move to a more easily defendable position, we needed somewhere to lie up during the daylight hours. Eventually we found a suitable site with high ground east, west and south of us and a dirt track to the north. So we established a base, moved our vehicles into a defensive position, put sentries to cover possible enemy approach routes and settled down to rest and prepare for the next night's reconnaissance. Unfortunately, because the map isn't the territory, we had unknowingly placed ourselves between two enemy posts and our sentries reported back that we were surrounded and massively outnumbered.

By late afternoon, the enemy had moved towards two vantage points. One of the groups occupied the high ground to the west, providing fire support to the group coming from the north, who were now advancing towards us in a flanking manoeuvre. Thanks to our sentries, we'd prepared ourselves and within moments of the enemy reaching our defensive positions, we engaged each other with small arms fire. We had a wounded soldier on the very first volley of fire. This didn't change anything; it was merely an obstacle that needed to be overcome. We needed to get out of this, regroup and then get back on track.

We were now in the pressure zone, surrounded and taking heavy fire from the enemy to the west and from the attack from the north. But we knew what to do – because we'd done it a thousand times before: 'basic' soldiering and contact drills. Each man knew his purpose and did it to the best of his ability. I just had to do my job as everyone else was doing theirs. I did not have to look left or right or behind me, because I already knew what the others were doing. In the military, we know where the competition is, and it is not internal, it is always external.

On a number of occasions, groups within the team called for support to help defend certain positions and it was given without question and unconditionally. When I needed extra men to deal with an attack to a flank, it was given to me instantly.

We had stopped the main attack and suppressed the group on the hill to our west. We had defended our position, but you can't win from defence alone. So now we attacked in order to open up a gap to escape. We attacked as one and with absolute and overwhelming force. Everyone in position, everyone knowing the plan, everyone coordinated; large firepower down, fire then manoeuvre and within a short time, no more than twenty minutes, we had control of the battle.

Two calls were now made by senior people of the same rank who were looking at the same situation from slightly different perspectives. One wanted us to leave the area straight away, leaving equipment we would find difficult to pack, such as our camouflage nets. The other wanted us to pack everything up as we had always done in practice. There was no right answer; each proposed action had its own merits.

This could have caused confusion and delay, but because both commanders were calm and knew each other's style, one said: 'Our best time to pack things away is fifteen minutes. We don't have fifteen minutes; we should leave.' With this simple explanation, the other commander said: 'Makes sense, let's go.' We proceeded to carry out the same drill we had done many times before, adapted slightly to allow for a spare arm around the wounded man. Each man now jumped onto their vehicle, moving into position to support the other vehicles by firing and manoeuvring until we were out of that situation. And then we were gone. One man down, but no lives lost. And a lot of chaos left in our wake. Job done.

I am often asked: how do you feel in this type of situation? I can honestly say the word 'focused' is the first that springs to my mind, because I can look around and see that my team are equally focused, working with and for each other. The wounded man gets life-saving attention; people give the thumbs-up to one another when a good decision is made; someone makes a quip that breaks the tension. In that moment we are in total harmony, in flow and working as one unit. We are also in solution mode: we will analyse the situation later, for now we must take action. The team's compass is aligned. Later in the battle when there was a lull, my thoughts did flicker to my family back in the UK, but my mind instantly removed them, with my brisk internal voice saying, 'NOT NOW! Stay focused and you will see them later.' Our basic drills gave us a great platform to work from.

We had all worked together prior to this deployment – for a number of months for the newest members, and years for the oldest. While we weren't all close friends, we respected each other enormously (liking people in a team is a nicety, not a necessity). And we all wanted to be there. Most soldiers are in their late twenties when they join the SAS, which means they come with experience. The selection process meant we all had a common standard of soldiering. And coming from different backgrounds, we had different physical capabilities and talents: among us were paramedics, engineers, scientists, teachers, mechanics, linguists, demolitionists. Diversity was our strength but, ultimately, we were a team.

So the principles of the Compass for Life are as important for a team as they are for an individual when it comes to achieving success. Most of the successful teams with which I have been associated all had a perfectly aligned team compass: a common purpose, an agreed ethos, a well-planned strategy and a warrior spirit to execute it.

Points for action: uniting your team

Do you have the key components of an elite team? As before, score yourself out of 10, with 10 being perfect, and avoid using the number 7.

You and your teammates respect one another ☐

You take the time to get to know your teammates ☐

You and your teammates support one another ☐

You are willing to apologise to one another if one of you drops the ball ☐

You are willing to acknowledge one another's skill and expertise ☐

You are able to talk about your strengths and weaknesses as a team ☐

You are able to engage in passionate debate in order to find solutions for the good of the team ☐

You are willing to challenge your teammates if they do not adhere to the code of conduct ☐

Your team is fully focused on the purpose ☐

Your team is agreed upon the correct strategy ☐

Your team focuses on what is best for the team first and foremost, before the needs of individuals ☐

Your team has a reputation for delivery ☐

Your team wants to leave a legacy of high performance ☐

Every member of your team is fully committed to the success of your objectives ☐

If you scored 0–4 in any area, that is a danger zone and must be improved, as it is a weak area for you and will undermine your performance. If you scored 5–7, there is room for improvement. If you scored 8–10, you're doing well!

Now calculate your overall average and the same rules apply.

If your team is not operating as a cohesive unit, consider what could be holding you back. Is there one particular member of the team who is letting the rest down? Could the relationships between all members be improved? Do you need to build increased levels of trust in the team? Is everyone pushing themselves to the absolute limits of their physical and mental abilities?

The more you can build a sense of team spirit and camaraderie, the closer your team will work together; and the more aligned the team compass becomes, the closer it gets to achieving its purpose.

Conclusion

To finish the story of my journey so far, let me explain where I am with my current Super North Star. Our virtual academy has been running for a year and the experiential leadership part has begun. We don't yet have a permanent location for the academy, but I can picture it all very clearly in my mind:

I look out of the window of the wooden cabin. It is a beautiful location, with a lake to the west and a forest surrounding us and seven other log cabins. I watch the very first group from Syndicate One start to climb the high wires to the aerial assault courses that tower above. I walk across to the operation room to listen to Tom barking out orders to the surveillance teams that are on the ground during one of the leadership exercises. The other cabins are full of students taking part in entrepreneurial challenges or another international negotiators' course. There is a buzz of excitement and nervous energy throughout the camp.

This is exactly how I imagine it will look in the future, and my current life map (opposite) has a picture of it in the top right-hand corner to keep me on track. I also have my timeline fully planned out and the first milestones clearly identified, with potential obstacles marked as well. I have started to move towards the first two milestones.

We have developed our strategy by collaborating with numerous experts who are also supporting the project, and we have Taunton in Somerset lined up to become the first Compass for Life town by September 2016. We have clear milestones and contingencies in place to deal with any obstacles that crop up. The ethos of the team is based on the desire to push the potential of every course member, from the youngest child to the oldest business person, through clear communication and a building of trust, ambition and confidence to push the bounds of their performance and leave a legacy for others to follow. I am very fortunate to have a number of warriors to support me on my journey and the great thing is that my Super North Star is also theirs – we are a team.

Once the academy is up and running, I already know what I want to turn my attention to next: taking this project overseas. I want to enable children around the world to experience the benefit of having a Compass for Life. I want to create a charity and send as many teachers as I can to follow through on this purpose. I think that would be a nice legacy to leave.

The Compass for Life is exactly that; it is a way to support our dreams and ambitions, whatever they are, throughout our lives, and it adjusts accordingly as our purpose changes. All we need to do is ensure that all the components of our compass are aligned.

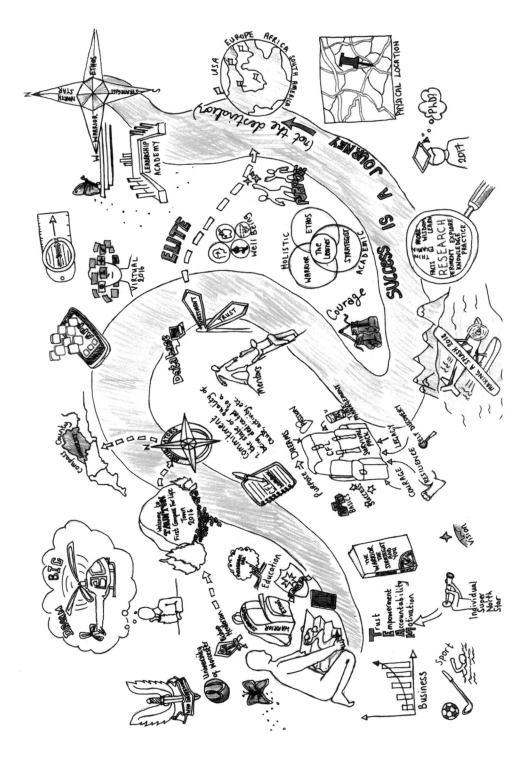

I hope that this book has inspired you and given you the confidence to start reaching for what you really want in life; that you can take the principles of the Compass for Life and start to apply them to your own circumstances.

Have the confidence to dream big, without fear of what others think, and start thinking of a purpose that has real meaning to you, one that is worth pursuing wholeheartedly. Remember to look at your current circumstances to assess your starting point, your skills, strengths and weaknesses, so that you know how to begin your journey. Identify the values that need to influence all the decisions and actions you take. Make sure you won't live to regret the way you have handled a situation, that your own behaviour won't hold you back from success. Never neglect your strategic side: once you have your goal in place, break down the steps you need to take to get there, prepare for the unknown, and give yourself enough facts to make informed decisions. But once you have that information, don't forget to take action. Approach everything you do with passion, determination and discipline so that you give it your best shot. Don't fear failure: treat it as a learning experience, a way to improve your performance so that you can succeed next time.

And above all, make sure that your compass is aligned: always consider every cardinal point as you progress along your journey, to make sure you are accounting for your Ethos, making use of your Strategist, embracing your inner Warrior, and heading firmly towards your final purpose, your Super North Star. Keep your life map with you to help you visualise your journey, inspire you and keep you focused on your end goal. Add to it, adapt it, but never forget to refer to it.

Remember, it's not all down to you. The people around you are key to your development and success. You are the sum of your parts, of the people who've helped make you and continue to support you on your journey. Make sure you know who these people are and keep them with you. I couldn't have made it this far without mine. We can be the best we can be on our own, but without our support network it will be that much tougher to succeed in life.

It is now time to hand over the story to you. Before I do, I would like to point out that people have said to me in the past: 'Look, Floyd, you were a Special Forces soldier, you're fit, strong and smart; it must have been easy for you.'

How I wish that were true! What those people had not seen – but you now know – are the hours of practice, the coming back from failure and the constant learning that is required. I've also had to deal with the same inner voices and fears as everyone else.

So let me leave you with these final thoughts:

- Dream big.

- Ignore those who try to knock you off your course.

- Keep your dreams alive in your head and heart and follow them with passion.

- Strive, practise, believe in yourself – and capture your star.

I wish you well on your journey. Good luck, have fun, and please let me know how you get on.

Final points for action: taking your next steps

☛ What does success look like in the next six months if you are to start moving towards your Super North Star? Visualise the results you want.

☛ What actions must you take and complete in the next three months to make this happen?

☛ What support do you need?

☛ Look at your map, and ask yourself: is it truly big and scary? Do you see yourself at the end of your journey and smile? Do you see happiness in your relationships with friends and family? Do you see your ideal career? Do you see yourself healthy and energised? Will you gain skills to be proud of? Will you be giving something back to your community or society? Will your journey, ultimately, be truly fulfilling?

Acknowledgements

M any people have helped me on my journey so far.
My mum and dad were my earliest inspiration. They taught by example the importance of hard work, self-sacrifice and resilience. Moving us to Alderney, when faced with opportunity, was a courageous risk. And their support – both obvious and subtle – did much to ensure that I, and all my siblings, succeeded on our chosen paths. And let's not forget competition! Whether in the ring or playing cards, I learned that competition was good, that failure is a learning opportunity and that endless practice is best of all.

I had some phenomenal teachers who supported and challenged me, told me to believe in myself and made me (sometimes unwillingly) learn skills and knowledge I still use today. But I also saw the damage that teachers can do; a silly comment that may seem funny or an offhand remark can undermine someone's confidence and throw a person, particularly a young person, off course for years and, in some cases, for life. From them, I learned how to protect my dreams.

In the boxing ring, from my competitors, I learned to deal with fear, to realise there is nothing wrong with being scared – it keeps us sharp and reminds us we're alive. It is our ability to deal with it and still step into the arena that counts.

From my friends I learned the true value of friendship. Many have become mentors from whom I can seek help and guidance when necessary. They are there in my hour of need and ask for nothing in return. These people are what part of life is really all about.

From Al Slater, I learned that advanced training is doing the basics extremely well. I learned to live the lessons he taught.

I'll never forget Suzanne Hudson, who taught me chess aged ten. From her I learned to defend the queen (ensure you, your team and organisation are healthy and secure) and capture the king (increase market share and beat the competition), a lesson I've only realised the worth of in the last six months. Imagine if I'd realised it when I was ten. We are surrounded by key thoughts – we just need to grasp them.

A figure who continues to provide me with inspiration is Alexander the Great. To be at the vanguard of his men, out-think his opposition and relentlessly pursue his dreams, as he did, inspired me as a child and still does today. He is why I never underestimate the power of young people to change the world.

Acknowledgements

My Hells Angels friends who ... well, that one is between us and perhaps for another book.

The list of initials below are also of people I have been inspired by and, in many cases, continue to be so: CD/BW/ST/RW/RW/JW/VO/SJ/BM/TM/SW/CT/RL/DC/PD/PL/AS/JT/PC/JL/JS/MC-S/RP/DT/KM/SH

Bibliography and Further Reading

I have come across many books that have helped me to develop this book, and ones that you may find interesting as further reading on strategies for success:

Buzan, Tony, and Keene, Raymond, *Buzan's Book of Genius* (London: Hutchinson, 1994)

Carnegie, Dale, *How to Win Friends and Influence People* (New York: Simon & Schuster, 1936)

Cialdini, Robert B., *Influence: Science and Practice* (Boston: Pearson Education, 2009)

Curran, Andrew, and Gilbert, Ian, ed., *Little Book of Big Stuff About the Brain* (Carmarthen: Crown House Publishing, 2008)

Gelb, Michael J., *Discover Your Genius* (New York: Harper Collins, 2002)

Hawkes, Neil, *How to Inspire and Develop Positive Values in the Classroom* (Manchester: LDA, 2003)

Kerr, James, *Legacy* (London: Constable, 2013)

Millman, Dan, *The Way of the Peaceful Warrior* (Tiburon, CA: H. J. Kramer, 2000)

Precht, Richard David, *Who Am I? And If So, How Many?* (New York: Spiegel & Grau, 2011)

Taylor, John; Furnham, Adrian; and Breeze, Janet, *Revealed: Using Remote Personality Profiling to Influence, Negotiate and Motivate* (London: Palgrave Macmillan, 2014)

Index

A

Adams, John Quincy 184
aerobic fitness 102, 129, 130
Alderney 142
Aldershot 144
Alexander the Great 6, 135–136, 177, 182, 202
Ali, Muhammad 120
All Blacks 177
Aristotle 104, 135
Armstrong, Lance 53
Athena 19
Atlantic Ocean 155–160
Aurelius, Marcus 49, 52, 149

B

basic(s)
  getting the basics right 103–105, 123, 124, 130, 169, 190, 191
  skills 103, 124
Baumgartner, Felix 17
body language 87, 95
body-kinaesthetic awareness 30, 40
Bradford 45–49, 142

Brasidas of Sparta 153
Brecon Beacons 14
Browning, Robert 11
Bucephalus 135–136
Buchan, John 179
Buddha 127

C

calm
  remaining 76, 116, 148, 181
Chesterton, G. K. 155
Cialdini, Robert 85
commitment 181–184
communication 19, 92, 163, 169, 173, 177, 179
  and negotiation 80–92
  vital under pressure 169
Compass for Life 3, 13–16. 51, 99, 168, 175, 178, 192, 194, 196, 198
  balancing our 137–139
  balancing your compass points 162–164
  in action 133–164
  team compass 168–170

contingencies 116
    planning for 80–92
courage 51, 113, 155, 157, 173,
    180–182
Curie, Marie 145

D
Dalí, Salvador 5
dance 102, 130
data
    analysing 72–79
discipline 111, 124, 155, 180, 182, 198
    self-discipline 128
    staying disciplined 110–111
dreams 3, 5, 21
    daydreaming 3, 5
    nurturing our 6–7

E
Einstein, Albert ix, 19, 180
Eisenhower, Dwight D. 77, 186
Ellington, Duke 30
emotions
    controlling our 68, 72, 74, 88–89,
        145, 150–153
    emotional intelligence 16, 45, 80, 169
    see also inner voice *and* mind
England 17, 120
Estabrook, Robert 83
ethos viii, 16, 19, 41–61, 75, 135, 138,
    158, 162, 170, 174, 175, 177, 188,
    192, 196, 198
    defining your 58–60
    failure 187
    SAS 57
    the people who shape our 44–49

F
failure 118, 145–146, 148, 198
    accept failure and learn from it
        118–119

fear 144–146, 149, 152, 155, 158, 160,
    161, 163, 198
    the greatest obstacle to success
        144–151
first impressions 95
flow 110, 191
focus 132, 181, 191, 193
    finding our 153–161
Frost, David 86

G
Gandhi, Mahatma 117
Gladwell, Malcolm 13, 74

H
health and well-being 100–103, 122,
    123, 129, 182
    see also aerobic fitness
heroes 6, 21, 27, 31, 112, 132, 135
    see also Alexander the Great
Horace 113
Hudson, Suzanne 67, 202

I
India 135
inner voice 20, 32, 67, 111–113,
    148–149, 161, 199
    see also mind
inspiration
    seizing 11–13
interpersonal skills 31, 40
intuition
    using our 116–118

J
Jefferson, Thomas 43
Jersey 142

K
Kennedy, John F. 89
Kennett, Dr Rob 179

Kenya 147
Kerr, James 177

L
Lao-Tzu 28, 115
leadership 38, 178–182, 184–188
    bad leadership 184–188
    good leadership 182–184, 188–191
legacy 22, 23, 43, 53, 76, 77, 194
Leonardo da Vinci 138, 141
life map ix, 96, 131, 164, 196, 197, 200
    creating a 16–18
listening 181
London 71, 117–118, 152

M
Macedonia 135
meditation 103, 131
mentors 14–15, 39, 44, 46, 48, 49, 132,
    174
    and guides 34–35
    see also Slater, Al
mind
    decluttering the 103, 131, 154, 157
    training our 111–113, 150
    see also inner voice
Moltke (the Elder), Helmuth von 72
Morrison, Lieutenant General David 187
motivation
    find our 32–33
multinational force 83–84, 87

N
Napoleon 5, 71
negotiation 90, 167, 179
    communication and 80 – 92
North Star, Super viii, 52, 96, 123, 132,
    135, 142, 144, 161, 188, 195, 196,
    198, 200
    finding our 1–24
    identifying 20–24

O
opportunities
    seize 139–144

P
Parachute Regiment 7, 13–14, 17, 49, 121,
    123, 143–144, 151–152, 158, 182
patience 106
performance
    pushing our 113–115
Philip, King (of Macedon) 135
Pilates 102, 130
plans/planning 28, 65, 67–68, 77–79,
    137
    adapting 72, 77–78, 84, 144
    for contingencies 79–80, 84, 104,
    116, 160
Portland 147
potential
    pushing our 28–30
power songs 131
practising 105–108
pressure
    communication vital under 169
    peer group 145
    training 108–110
    zone 127, 169, 190
purpose 20, 23, 38, 39, 56, 75, 84, 92,
    94, 173–176, 188, 192–194
    adapting our 7–10
    the power of 5–6

R
rest 103, 131
role play 95, 107, 171
Rosten, Leo 173

S
SAS x, 7–8, 14, 17, 29, 56, 65–67, 107,
    120, 122–123, 138, 147, 149, 158,
    167, 168, 170, 172, 174, 178, 192

Scandinavia 182
Schutz, Peter 171
Scotland 124
Shakespeare, William 53
Sitting Bull 99
Slater, Al 14–15, 49–50, 105, 202
sleep 103, 129
starting point
    assessing your 36
    establishing our 25–40
strategist/strategy viii, 15, 19, 63–96,
        135, 136, 137, 138, 139, 155, 162,
        174, 188, 192, 193, 198
    defending your strategic side
        69–72
    developing your strategic side
        93–96
    'shadow strategists' 78
    strengths and weaknesses 96
    the importance of 67–68
success
    fear as the greatest obstacle to
        144–151
    the path to 188–192
Sun Tzu 182
support network
    our personal 167–168
Sutton Coldfield 143
Swithenbank, J. W. 47

T
taking your next steps 200
Taunton 196
team(s) 60, 61, 66, 74, 75, 79, 80, 85,
        90, 109, 114–115, 127, 138, 158,
        164, 196
    bringing team members together
        174–178
    ethos 55–57
    leadership see 38, 178–191
    selecting our 170–174
    spirit 194
    uniting your 193–194
    working as a 165–194
Tecumseh, Chief 170
Thurman, Howard
Toffler, Alvin x
training 169, 183
Trigger, Major Dick 182–183
Twain, Mark 31, 143, 154

V
values
    knowing our 51–53
    sticking to our 53–55

W
Wales 124
warlord, meeting with 83–92
warrior viii, 16, 19, 65, 96–132,
        135–139, 162, 170, 174, 175, 177,
        188, 192, 196, 198
    strengthening your warrior side
        127–132
Weston-on-the-Green 151
Wilkinson, Jonny 17

Y
yoga 102, 130

Z
zones (white, green, amber, red) 132, 154